TIMEI

CW00811717

HORSES TO FULLUW

2013 FLAT SEASON

CONTENTS

TIMEFORM

© **TIMEFORM LIMITED 2013**
COPYRIGHT AND LIABILITY

ISBN 978 1 901570 89 2   Price £9.95

Printed and bound by
Charlesworth Press,
Wakefield, UK 01924 204830

SECTION

Timeform's Fifty To Follow, carefully chosen by members of Timeform's editorial staff, are listed below with their respective page numbers. A selection of ten (**marked in bold with a** ★) is made for those who prefer a smaller list.

The form summary for each horse is shown after its age, colour, sex and pedigree. The summary shows the distance, the state of the going and where the horse finished in each of its races on the Flat during 2012. Performances are in chronological sequence with the date of its last race shown at the end.

The distance of each race is given in furlongs, fractional distances being expressed in the decimal notation to the nearest tenth of a furlong. Races run in Britain on all-weather surfaces are prefixed by 'f' for fibresand and 'p' for polytrack.

The going is symbolised as follows: f=firm (turf) or fast (all-weather); m=good to firm (turf) or standard to fast (all-weather); g=good (turf) or standard (all-weather), d=good to soft/dead (turf) or standard to slow (all-weather); s=soft (turf) or slow (all-weather); v=heavy.

Placings are indicated, up to the sixth place, by use of superior figures, an asterisk being used to denote a win.

The Timeform Rating of a horse is simply the merit of the horse expressed in pounds and is arrived at by careful examination of its running against other horses. The ratings range from 130+ for tip-top classic performers down to a figure of around 20 for the poorest. Symbols attached to the ratings: 'p'–likely to improve; 'P'–capable of much better form; '+'–the horse may be better than we have rated it.

Absolutely So (Ire) 87p
3 b.c Acclamation – Week End (Selkirk (USA))
2012 6.5v³ p6m* Nov 21

Owners Jackie and George Smith may have enjoyed notable success with the very smart Royal Millennium around a decade ago but it seems that with the recent acquisition of some new silks—yellow with dark blue spots on sleeves—and the transfer of their horses to Andrew Balding they have sought to significantly upgrade the quality of their racecourse representatives. Race And Status, Soviet Rock and Absolutely So cost a combined 650,000 gns in 2011, and all three set about paying back their respective price tags with victories in their first season. The last-named looks especially interesting starting the new campaign from what could prove a very lenient opening BHA mark of 77.

Absolutely So showed bags of ability at the first time of asking when sent off joint-favourite for a maiden on heavy going at Newbury in late-October, a race in which he was found out by a lack of experience having refused to settle held up and run green when shaken up. That effort, beaten three quarters of a length into third behind Carry On Sydney, turned out to be fairly strong form, and Absolutely So didn't need to improve when landing the odds in a twelve-runner similar event on Lingfield's polytrack on his only subsequent start, in which he readily beat second favourite (and future winner) Whipper Snapper by a length and a quarter. Despite clearly being some way off the finished article, Absolutely So created a very positive impression with the way he travelled on both his outings, something which will surely stand him in good stead in the sprint handicaps he will be contesting as a three-year-old, and he could even end up better than a handicapper in time—he's from the family of Pass The Peace, Embassy and King's Apostle, all of whom were Group 1 winners at up to an extended six furlongs. ***Andrew Balding***

Jamie Lynch, Chief Correspondent (Absolutely So): *"It might not appear that I've delved too deeply into the book, and the pressure of handpicking one standout horse for the year inevitably leads to cold feet, but the only reason for cold feet in this case is because Absolutely So absolutely knocked socks off with his two runs last autumn. The first was the better form, but the second was the real eye-opener, when he pulled all the way around Lingfield and still ran right away at the finish, looking a horse who'll really sock it to 'em in 2013. Should I put a sock in it now and just say he'll win good races? Absolutely so."*

Alcaeus   –p
3 b.c Hernando (Fr) – Alvarita (Selkirk (USA))
2012 p7g p7g⁴ p7f Aug 30

Sir Mark Prescott has caused more scratching of heads than Ernő Rubik (the creator of the famous cube), with the Baronet perennially setting handicappers, bookmakers and punters posers as to whether his thrice-raced runners are the proverbial blot on the handicap or simply a blot on the landscape at Heath House Stables. Alcaeus may not have shown much in terms of solid form so far but he has all the credentials of an archetypal Prescott improver at three years, with his breeding pointing to him taking off once stepped up to middle distances.

Prescott, who famously once rejected Sheikh Mohammed's request to train some of his horses because he was loath to govern a string of more than fifty, gave Alcaeus three races inside a month as a juvenile, all over seven furlongs on the polytrack at Kempton. Although beaten at least a dozen lengths on each start—

his best effort came when fourth of nine to Royal Prize—Alcaeus nevertheless showed a glimpse of ability on each occasion, staying on from the rear in the style of a horse whose forte is stamina not speed. Alcaeus cost 43,000 gns as a yearling and has an appealing pedigree, being a brother to the useful Albert Bridge who was a very progressive performer at up to two miles for Ralph Beckett in 2012. Their dam Alvarita, a Prescott-trained mile-and-a-quarter winner who is out of the trainer's dual Champion Stakes winner Alborada, has also produced Alla Speranza, who won a Group 3 over a mile and a quarter in Ireland in the latest season. Given his profile, it's not hard to envisage Alcaeus proving a different proposition once sent handicapping over more suitable trips, and he should certainly be able to rack up a few wins from a modest opening mark. *Sir Mark Prescott Bt*

Asgardella (Ire) 83p
3 b.f Duke of Marmalade (Ire) – Peaceful Kingdom (USA) (King of Kings (Ire))
2012 7.2m* 7f² 6m⁵ 7s Oct 6

Despite having eleven runners spread across the Gold, Silver and Bronze Cups at Ayr on the fourth Saturday in September, as well as a group-race contender in Mary's Daughter, in his blog Richard Fahey actually nominated Asgardella each-way in a sales race at Newmarket as his bet of the day—'we like this filly a lot' said the trainer. Asgardella could finish only fifth but, as in her three other races as a two-year-old, her effort suggested she could prove a different proposition when tackling handicaps over further this season.

From the first crop of King George winner Duke of Marmalade, and the second foal of an unraced half-sister to the smart performer up to a mile and a half Magistretti, the Middleham Park Racing-owned Asgardella is bred to be suited by at least a mile, and with that in mind, it's encouraging that she showed fairly useful form at up to seven furlongs in her first year. Successful in an Ayr maiden on her debut, Asgardella's best performance came when three and a quarter lengths second in a nursery at York (BHA mark of 73), with the form of the race working out very well subsequently. The winner, conceding just 5 lb to Asgardella, was future Oh So Sharp Stakes heroine Waterway Run, while two lengths behind Asgardella in third was I'm Back, winner of a nursery off a mark of 83 on his next outing. Asgardella was far from disgraced in a couple of valuable sales races at Newmarket won by Victrix Ludorum after, each time looking ready for a step up in trip. A mile and further will suit Asgardella in the new season, when we fully expect her to make her mark in handicaps. *Richard Fahey*

Biographer ★   114p

4 b.c Montjeu (Ire) – Reflective (USA) (Seeking The Gold (USA))
2012 10v² 12d* p13g² 12s* 14d² 14s* Oct 5

The portents are good for Biographer developing into a Cup horse this term. Biographer emulated another colt who failed to make the track as a two-year-old in the Sir Michael Stoute-trained Ask when runner-up in the Melrose Handicap (beaten three and a half lengths by Guarantee) at York in August, and his win in the listed Noel Murless Stakes at Ascot on his final start meant comparisons could be drawn with John Dunlop's Akmal, who had landed both races in 2009. Ask would develop into a high-class performer as a four-year-old, winning the Ormonde and Cumberland Lodge Stakes, while Akmal won the Henry II at Sandown. With Biographer's Timeform rating 2 lb higher than the one awarded to Akmal at the same stage in his career—Ask began his second season rated 116—and a step up to two miles promising to suit, he is fancied make his mark in some of the better staying races this season.

After just six starts Biographer is already up there with the best horses David Lanigan, who moved to Kingsdown Stables in Lambourn last August, has trained since saddling his first runner in 2008; Derby runner-up Main Sequence is rated 119, while subsequently-disqualified Oaks second Meeznah reached 115 at her peak. Biographer, who also won a maiden at Doncaster and a handicap at Ffos Las in 2012, elevated his form to smart when beating next-time-out listed-race winner Sir Graham Wade at Ascot in a contest that, for all it was a steadily-run, looks worth following. Biographer did well to overcome a positional bias having been waited with that day and, after quickening to lead a furlong out, he fairly stormed clear despite drifting right—all in all it was a performance that suggested Biographer still has plenty of chapters left to fill. The useful-looking Biographer acts on polytrack, and has raced only on going softer than good on turf. *David Lanigan*

Blessing Box   66p

3 b.f Bahamian Bounty – Bible Box (Ire) (Bin Ajwaad (Ire))
2012 5g p6f p5g² Oct 31

Following Chris Wall's three-year-old handicappers blind over the last five seasons would have accrued a profit of £62.46 to a £1 level stake, while supporting the trainer's sprinter of a few years back Bounty Box in each of her eighteen starts would have also left you in the black. Now it's the turn of her sister Blessing Box to continue the winning streak.

Blessing Box has a certain amount to live up to as both Bounty Box and her other sister Charity Box won at least one handicap early on in their careers; Bounty Box won off BHA marks of 78 and 86 before going on to prove herself smart as a four- and five-year-old, while Charity Box (unraced at two) scored off a mark of 65 on her handicap bow over seven furlongs last June. Blessing Box showed just modest form in a trio of maidens in 2012 but the overriding impression was that she had plenty more to offer, shaping better than the result on each occasion. Having finished nearer last than first in races at Sandown and Kempton, Blessing Box went much closer when one and a half lengths second to shock winner Multitask at Lingfield, a race in which she was left with a lot to do and stayed on in eye-catching fashion in the hands of Ted Durcan. We believe Blessing Box is capable of emulating her siblings this season, when she will start off in sprint handicaps from an official rating of 64. *Chris Wall*

Bowland Princess 63p
3 b.f Tiger Hill (Ire) – Kozmina (Ire) (Sadler's Wells (USA))
2012 8.3g 8.3d p8.6g⁵ Oct 18

Ed Dunlop has enjoyed success at the highest level with the likes of Ouija Board, Snow Fairy and Red Cadeaux in recent years, but do you recall that the last-named actually gained his first win in a 0-80 event at Wolverhampton? Red Cadeaux would pick up a further three handicaps before landing his first pattern race. It remains to be seen whether Bowland Princess can ever reach such heights, but she will begin life in handicaps off a lowly mark and it will be disappointing if she cannot pay her way.

Owned by the partnership of Lowe, Silver and Deal who have enjoyed success with the smart Rhythm of Light and modest three-time handicap winner at up to two miles Mina's Boy (a Sinndar half-brother to this filly), Bowland Princess showed plenty of promise in three juvenile maidens despite running to just a modest level. In keeping with both her pedigree and physique—she's a big, raw filly—Bowland Princess simply wasn't sharp enough to contest the business end of races over an extended mile, and this was summed up by her run at Wolverhampton on her final outing. Having recovered from dwelling at the start to race in mid-field, Bowland Princess caught the eye with the way she made headway over a furlong out but was unable to go with the principals in the closing stages, with jockey Tom McLaughlin not persevering once her chance had gone. The seventh foal of an unraced half-sister to the dam of High Chaparral who has produced two more winners aside from Mina's Boy, all aspects of Bowland Princess' profile suggest she'll do more to enhance the family name at three, when middle distances will suit her well. *Ed Dunlop*

Bright Strike (USA) 88p
3 b.c Smart Strike (Can) – Seebe (USA) (Danzig (USA))
2012 7m³ 7g³ 7m² Sep 22

In terms of both number of winners (eighteen) and total prize money (£622,142) George Strawbridge enjoyed his most fruitful year as an owner in Britain in 2012. The year also saw the American educator, historian, investor, sportsman and philanthropist record his first Royal Ascot victory courtesy of Gatewood in the Wolferton Handicap, while Aiken and Thought Worthy won five races between them, including a pair of Group 2s. Strawbridge looks set for another successful season in 2013, with Bright Strike appealing as one who could contribute handsomely.

Bright Strike showed plenty of promise in three starts in maidens as a two-year-old, all of which look strong form. Ahead of a clutch of subsequent winners when third to Timoneer at Newmarket on his debut, he finished two places ahead of another member of our *Fifty*, Greeleys Love, when filling the same position behind Wentworth at York, and confirmed himself a useful prospect at Newbury on his final start. Sent off a shade of odds on in a field of eighteen, Bright Strike was headed a furlong out having made the running but kept on pleasingly, simply unlucky to bump into a good prospect in Race And Status, who would go on to finish third to Bright Strike's stablemate Ghurair in a hot sales race. The sturdy and attractive Bright Strike was bred by Strawbridge and is a half-brother to several winners, notably the same owner's 2011 two-year-old mile winner Gathering and mile-and-a-quarter winner Seelo, both useful. Sure to be well suited by at least a mile himself—his sire has produced the likes of at least very smart performers at up to a mile and a half Curlin and English Channel in the States, and smart stayer Tungsten Strike in this country—Bright Strike can improve further as a three-year-old and win a handicap or two. *John Gosden*

Burning Blaze ★ 95p
3 b.c Danroad (Aus) – Demeter (USA) (Diesis)
2012 7.2s³ 6f* 6g 6v³ Oct 12

A £47.31 profit to a £1 level stake would have been the result of following all of Kevin Ryan's Flat runners over the last two years, and there seems no reason why the good times shouldn't continue in 2013, with Burning Blaze one of those looking set to make an even greater contribution. The first horse trained by Ryan for Sheikh Fahad Al Thani's Qatar Racing, whose racing manager David Redvers part-bred the colt, Burning Blaze appeals as a sprint handicapper who will waste little time in proving himself better than his current BHA mark of 86.

The form of Burning Blaze's first two outings worked out very well, separating two next-time-out winners when third to Elnadancer in a maiden at Ayr in July and beating no fewer than six future scorers headed by the useful Cour Valant when landing a nine-runner similar race at York three weeks later. In his two subsequent starts, again on the Knavesmire, Burning Blaze was ridden by Jamie Spencer, who is now retained as first jockey to Sheikh Fahad. Having been given a seven-week break after blotting his copybook when sent off favourite for a competitive nursery in August, Burning Blaze fared much better when third to Polski Max in a similar event, looking ahead of his mark with the way he travelled but seeming to find the emphasis on stamina in the testing conditions against him. A further pointer to his prospects at three is his pedigree. A 75,000-guinea breeze-up purchase, Burning Blaze is a half-brother to Chris Wall's 2010 Chartwell Stakes winner Pyrrha, who was effective at up to seven furlongs (should have stayed a mile) and who improved significantly from two to three, landing a brace of handicaps in her second season. With such strong form to his name and good prospects of further improvement, we believe that Burning Blaze, whose best effort to date has come over six furlongs, will be well worth following in the new season. *Kevin Ryan*

Captain Cat (Ire) ★   100p
4 b.g Dylan Thomas (Ire) – Mother of Pearl (Ire) (Sadler's Wells (USA))
2012 8s³ 8g* 8d² Oct 5

Standing over sixteen hands high it's not surprising that Roger Charlton joked that Captain Cat could one day make a chaser, but we think he has plenty more to offer on the level yet. A May foal who was given five months off prior to his final start in 2012 in order to strengthen and mature, Captain Cat has the profile of a horse who could take his already useful form to the next level in 2013.

Once-raced at two years, Captain Cat built on his return (third to subsequent Gordon Stakes winner Noble Mission) when beating the now useful Lahaag by a comfortable four and a half lengths in a thirteen-runner maiden on Newmarket's Rowley Mile in May. It was a performance that suggested more to come from the Seasons Holidays-owned winner, especially as he was still a bit green off the bridle, edging right when taking it up over a quarter of a mile from home. Captain Cat wasn't seen out again until the autumn and duly improved a bit further when a length second of nine to another useful sort in Jake's Destiny in a minor event at Ascot, again impressing with the way he travelled (looked the likeliest winner when looming up two furlongs out) but finding only the one pace for pressure. Raced only at a mile so far, on pedigree Captain Cat should stay further—he's by Dylan Thomas and out of a mare who stayed a mile and a half, whilst his close relative Danehill's Pearl (by Danehill Dancer) was a useful winner over a mile and a quarter—though as a strong traveller it could be that trips around a mile will suit for the time being. Either way, we think Captain Cat still has plenty of untapped potential heading into his four-year-old campaign, and he looks just the sort to win a good handicap, with the Hunt Cup striking as a suitable target. **Roger Charlton**

Pat Jupp, Handicapper (Captain Cat): *"Captain Cat improved with each run in a light campaign last year, impressing with his cruising speed, and more progress looks assured as he fills his considerable frame. It would be a surprise were he not able to take advantage of his opening mark, and he possesses the tools to be a major player in valuable handicaps over the summer, too."*

Danchai   95p

4 gr.g Authorized (Ire) – Scarlet Empire (Ire) (Red Ransom (USA))
2012 9.2v* 12s⁵ Oct 14

As the first foal of an unraced half-sister to smart performers Arctic (sprinter), Shanty Star (up to two miles) and Sky Lantern, who was herself out of a daughter of Negligent, the champion two-year-old filly in England in 1989, Danchai hails from a family of successful greys. Danchai himself hasn't reached the same level yet, but with just three runs behind him we have high hopes that he could progress to that standard in 2013.

Danchai's sole start as a juvenile (for David Lanigan) was full of promise, second to the now useful Kiz Kulesi and comfortably ahead of several subsequent winners, and he wasted little time in getting off the mark as a three-year-old, albeit not returning until late-September and having been gelded in the interim. Admittedly, Danchai had little to beat in that maiden at Hamilton—he landed the odds by nine lengths—but it still represented useful form, making an opening mark of 85 look more than fair ahead of a switch to handicaps. Danchai failed to come up to scratch sent to Goodwood for his handicap debut, only fifth of ten behind Nicholascopernicus, though it's possible the marked step up in trip was against him at that stage of his development. Still very much unexposed and in the care of a well-respected trainer, Danchai's potential remains undented, with the fact that he's been dropped 2 lb by the official assessor an added bonus for his prospects in the coming season. Raced only on good going or softer so far, Danchai should stay a mile and a quarter. **William Haggas**

Desert Command   76p
3 b.g Oasis Dream – Speed Cop (Cadeaux Genereux)
2012 6d p6f⁶ 6m Sep 21

There are a number of theories that seek to explain the notion of déjà vu, but for regular readers of this publication who are now experiencing that eerie feeling having scanned over the pedigree of Desert Command, we can solve the mystery for you—the last three editions of *Horses To Follow* have each featured an unexposed Andrew Balding-trained three-year-old out of Speed Cop, with Desert Command following his half-brother Top Cop (by Acclamation) a year ago and full brother Desert Law in 2011. Although Top Cop disappointingly failed to win a race in 2012, he and Desert Law (significantly so) were improved performers in their second season on the racecourse and we envisage Desert Command very much following suit.

Desert Command didn't manage to run to the same level as a two-year-old as those two siblings, but he displayed distinct promise in three maidens nonetheless. Never on terms at Salisbury on his debut, Desert Command's best effort came when four lengths sixth of eleven to Inka Surprise at Kempton, a race in which he showed the speed associated with his family by going with zest in a share of the lead until two furlongs out. Desert Command wasn't knocked about once his chance had gone that day and he again shaped as if not quite the finished article when down the field, albeit sandwiched between two next-time-out winners, at Newbury, following which he was gelded and put away for the year. Desert Law and Top Cop both began life in handicaps off a mark in the low-90s, but Desert Command, who looks to have inherited a share of his family's ability, will start 2013 off just 68 and should prove well up to winning races. He will prove best at five and six furlongs. **Andrew Balding**

Dick Bos 96p

4 ch.g Dutch Art – Cosmic Countess (Ire) (Lahib (USA))
2012 8s p7.1m^2 6s* Oct 8

Dick Bos may be sturdy in physique but he has evidently been difficult to train. The gelding, named by his original owners The Comic Strip Heroes after a fictional Dutch private eye who was not only proficient at martial arts but a crack shot who spoke at least half a dozen languages, was sufficiently highly regarded as a two-year-old to be given a Middle Park entry, but he failed to make the track that year and was absent for a further five months after a relatively low-key racecourse bow at Newbury last April. Dick Bos impressed significantly in two subsequent starts last term however, and, despite being sold out of Peter Chapple-Hyam's yard for 18,000 gns in November (he'd cost £48,000 as a yearling), he makes plenty of appeal heading into this campaign in the care of a trainer who is a dab hand at revitalising (and frequently improving) the cast-offs of others.

Dick Bos was well backed when resurfacing in a maiden at Wolverhampton in late-September and was unlucky not to land the odds, short of room and forced to switch out wide over a furlong out before finishing fast to be beaten a head. He made no mistake in a similar event back on turf at Windsor, where he again started favourite. Seemingly suited by the drop back to six furlongs (his sire and dam both put up their best performance over the trip), Dick Bos travelled strongly in touch then quickened clear from two furlongs out to beat fifteen rivals, headed by the fairly useful Lupo d'Oro, by over four lengths. Admittedly there probably wasn't much depth to the race but Dick Bos, a half-brother to three winners who include seventeen-furlong winner Lucky Diva and seven-furlong scorer Miss Madame, still looked an unusually promising sort to be found in a back-end maiden for three-year-olds and up. Set to race for the successful Middleham Park Racing syndicate this term, the highly progressive Dick Bos looks to have been let in lightly from an opening handicap mark of 80, even on the bare form of his maiden win, and remains open to improvement after just three starts. ***David O'Meara***

Enthusiastic 98

5 b.h Galileo (Ire) – Que Puntual (Arg) (Contested Bid (USA))
2012 12m^2 p12.2g* p12m* Sep 26

Michael Murphy reportedly first took out a licence to train in 1989, but the former jump jockey, who had been running a pre-training business in Newmarket for a number of years, saddled his first winner since becoming a fully-fledged trainer in 2012 when Enthusiastic landed a maiden at Wolverhampton in late-August.

Described as 'the best I've got' by the handler, Enthusiastic impressed again when following up in a handicap and looks one to keep on side this season.

Luca Cumani trained Mad Rush to win the 2008 Old Newton Cup, as well as the likes of Manighar and Sour Mash, for American businessman and former United States Ambassador to Finland Earle Mack, but the owner removed a clutch of his horses from the trainer in 2011. They included Enthusiastic who had shaped with some promise when fourth on his only start as a three-year-old for Cumani. After showing much improved form when runner-up on his belated return for his new stable at Newmarket, Enthusiastic confirmed he had more than his share of ability by going on to beat ten rivals at Wolverhampton a fortnight later, despite showing the odd sign of inexperience after he'd hit the front. Allotted a mark of 78, Enthusiastic went on to make a successful handicap debut at Kempton, where the winning margin of a length doesn't do anything like full justice to his superiority, the 11/4 favourite actually doing very well to lead inside the final fifty yards having been denied a run and shuffled back two furlongs out. After the race his trainer gave an indication as to the regard in which Enthusiastic is held, stating: 'I've got a few potential targets. One is a Group 3 over a mile and a half at Baden-Baden next month'. The lengthy Enthusiastic wasn't asked to take up his German assignment, which points to connections wanting to take advantage of his current mark of 86 before progressing to better things. He stays a mile and a half and is proven so far on polytrack and good to firm ground. *Michael Murphy*

Flow (USA)   88p
3 b.c Medaglia d'Oro (USA) – Enthused (USA) (Seeking The Gold (USA))
2012 7g⁴ 7m² 8g* Sep 20

Sir Michael Stoute trained the likes of very smart six- and seven-furlong performer Arakan, as well as Lowther winner Enthused and the smart Ea, for the Niarchos Family in the early part of this century, but he has saddled just two horses for the owner over the last three years, both without success. The owner's other long-standing trainer in Britain is Sir Henry Cecil, who this season will again be responsible for Flow, the seventh foal of Enthused, and a half-brother to several winners, including the aforementioned miler Ea.

Flow showed fairly useful form in three starts in maidens as a juvenile, ridden by stable jockey Tom Queally each time, with his best effort a neck second of seven to Tamayuz Star at Leicester in August. That form was franked in no uncertain terms when the winner finished runner-up in a listed contest and won a valuable sales race on his next two starts, while third Shebebi and fourth Lord of The Garter both won a race before the season was out. Five weeks later at Yarmouth the odds-on Flow broke his duck with the minimum of fuss, travelling fluently in front and keeping on to hold off Swing Easy by a length. That race didn't look the strongest at the time, but subsequent events, with the second, third and fourth all opening their accounts during the next month or two, suggest the form has a fair amount of substance to it, and Flow looks just the sort who will continue to go the right way as a three-year-old.

Flow holds a Derby entry, an indication that he's held in high regard, but both his pedigree (none of his siblings have won over further than a mile) and running style at two (smooth traveller) suggest trips short of a mile and a half will prove his optimum. Ea finished second in the Britannia on his third outing as a three-year-old, and that race could well be on Flow's agenda initially, with an opening BHA mark of 84 looking very inviting. He'll pay to follow. *Sir Henry Cecil*

Glorious Protector (Ire)   78P
3 b.c Azamour (Ire) – Hasaiyda (Ire) (Hector Protector (USA))
2012 8g⁶ Sep 27

In a July stable tour Ed Walker described Racing Post Trophy entry Glorious Protector as a 'lovely horse for the future … one to remember for next year' and later added on his website that the colt 'has a huge amount of class and athleticism'. Therefore, despite being sent off at 33/1 in a maiden at Newmarket, it probably came as no surprise to the trainer that Glorious Protector shaped so promisingly, looking like one who should have no problem taking a similar race en route to better things this season.

A useful-looking colt who had apparently been allowed time to fill into his large frame, Glorious Protector wasn't at all knocked about by Jamie Spencer when finishing sixth behind fellow *Horse To Follow* Telescope in what appeals as a well above-average affair, with fifth Soviet Rock and eighth Autun both winning next time. Dropped out early, Glorious Protector travelled smoothly and, after making good mid-race headway, looked to cross the line with plenty more to give, very much catching the eye of our man on the course. It was a performance that would have undoubtedly pleased his owner Ms Yap, in whose pink and royal blue braces the colt runs, though in other circumstances Glorious Protector could easily have found his rider wearing the rather more famous green with red epaulets of the Aga Khan. His sire sported the famous colours with distinction during his three seasons on the track, with the King George among his four Group 1 wins, and his dam was also owned by the Aga Khan during her racing career and at stud until sold in

2009 whilst carrying Glorious Protector. Unsurprisingly, Azamour's best progeny so far have improved appreciably from two to three (Colombian, Eleanora Duse and Laajooj to name just three) and we expect this colt to do exactly that in 2013, when a step up to middle distances will suit him well. **Ed Walker**

Gospel Choir ★   109p
4 ch.c Galileo (Ire) – Chorist (Pivotal)
2012 9.9g* 12g* 11.9m* 12f Sep 8

Mountain High, Class Is Class, Main Aim, Distinction, Heaven Sent and even the great Pilsudski; just some Sir Michael Stoute-trained horses who went on to scale the heights in pattern company having been rated inferior to Gospel Choir at the same stage in their careers. Heaven Sent, in the same ownership as Gospel Choir, was an especially slow burner having begun her four-year-old campaign with a Timeform rating of just 92 (she ended it rated 116) and, while it's asking a lot to expect the same level of improvement from Gospel Choir, it will be disappointing if he isn't playing a major part in pattern races come the second half of the campaign.

Gospel Choir gaining the last of his three wins in 2012

Having shown promise in his sole start as a juvenile, Gospel Choir quickly progressed into a useful performer in 2012, when he won a maiden at Salisbury and handicaps at Ascot in July and Haydock in August. The form of the last-named win proved particularly strong, with third-placed Sir Graham Wade, who was chasing a four-timer, landing two more good-quality handicaps and a listed race before the year was out. Gospel Choir was sent off clear favourite to end his campaign with victory in a very competitive three-year-old handicap back at Ascot but wasn't seen to best effect, travelling well behind the leaders when baulked two furlongs out and unable to recover. However, the strength of his previous form was still underlined, with the Haydock runner-up Stencive beaten just a neck into second by Ahzeemah.

Although by Coolmore's supersire Galileo, the well-made Gospel Choir is very much a product of Cheveley Park Stud's racing and breeding programme, with his dam, Chorist, one of their star performers in the early part of the century. Chorist progressed in each of her four seasons on the track, which is further reason to expect Gospel Choir to carry on improving as a four-year-old, when he can first win a good handicap before moving onto the bigger stage. Gospel Choir, who usually responds generously to pressure, promises to be suited by a step up to a mile and three quarters and acts on good to firm going (unraced on softer than good). *Sir Michael Stoute*

Greatwood ★   93p
3 b.c Manduro (Ger) – Gaze (Galileo (Ire))
2012 7g² 8s³ p8f* Oct 24

Luca Cumani trained Montendre to land the Rockingham Stakes as a juvenile and the eleven-time winner is now enjoying his retirement at Greatwood, a rescue and rehabilitation centre for ex-racehorses in Wiltshire. Among the other horses now housed at the centre are Poltergeist and Forgery, who both raced for the Highclere Throughbreds, and that syndicate's three-year-old colt Greatwood looks one of Cumani's brightest hopes for the new season after making a very positive start to his career in 2012.

Greatwood was unusually strong in the market for a debutant from his stable when backed down to 7/1 from an opening 16/1 for a maiden at Leicester in September, and he showed just why by finishing a promising second to subsequent winner Penny Rose, finishing well from the rear under hands and heels. The form of that race worked out well, as did Greatwood's second start when third to fellow member of the *Fifty* So Beloved at Salisbury, with future Horris Hill winner Tawhid splitting the pair. Greatwood didn't need to improve to open his account when beating next-time-out winner Stasio by a neck at Kempton on his third start, though he impressed with the way he overcame unfavourable circumstances having raced freely in mid-division in a slowly-run race, finishing strongly to take over close home. The fact that Derby entry Greatwood managed to win at all as a two-year-old bodes very well, as his pedigree suggests he will be suited by a step up to at least a mile and a quarter in 2013. By a sire in Manduro who was effective at up to a mile and a half, Greatwood is the second foal of German mile-and-a-quarter winner Gaze, a Galileo close relation to Irish Derby/Gold Cup winner Fame And Glory. The first foal, Bridgehampton, was a multiple winner at up to a mile and three quarters for Michael Bell in 2012.

With his trainer having saddled the likes of Franciscan, Aktia and Mabait to win a clutch of handicaps during their respective three-year-old campaigns over the last few seasons, it would be no surprise if Greatwood contributed generously to Bedford House's haul in 2013. *Luca Cumani*

Greeleys Love (USA)   87p
3 ch.c Mr Greeley (USA) – Aunt Winnie (Ire) (Deputy Minister (Can))
2012 7.2v^3 7.2m 7g^5 7d* Sep 18

A quick online search points to owner Mick Doyle having his fingers in plenty of pies as he is listed as a director of such limited companies as Doyle Fishing, Knockagorna Trading and Crookhavin Investments. Followers of Flat racing, however, may recognise another of Doyle's enterprises in County Donegal-based Crone Stud Farms, under which banner horses such as Greeleys Love run. Doyle had his first runner (in his own name) in Britain in 1992, but when Greeleys Love made his debut at Ayr in July he became the first horse carrying the owner's orange, emerald green stars to represent a trainer other than Mark Johnston.

The fact that Doyle went to $105,000 to purchase Greeleys Love as a yearling probably owes plenty to the fact that his dam, a lightly-raced maiden in the States, is a half-sister to Pearl of Love, who was victorious in Doyle's silks in the 2003 Group 1 Gran Criterium at Milan. Greeleys Love showed a fair level of ability in maidens, and his third effort, when fifth to Wentworth in a strong contest at York, suggested that his form could take off once switched to handicaps. Allotted a BHA mark of 72, Greeleys Love was sent off at 11/2 for a thirteen-runner nursery at Thirsk and duly progressed a chunk to beat Dr Phibes, though the bare margin of victory (three quarters of a length) didn't do him full justice. Having raced in mid-field for the most part, Philip Makin's mount did well to overcome interference a furlong out, and the form was given added substance when the second and third both won on their next respective outings. All in all, a 6 lb rise shouldn't trouble Greeleys Love, who strikes as a handicapper whose form to date almost certainly doesn't come close to reflecting the ceiling of his ability. Plenty of Mr

Greeley's most notable progeny—Finsceal Beo, Reel Buddy, Western Aristocrat for example—have excelled at around a mile and the unfurnished Greeleys Love looks set to follow suit. **Kevin Ryan**

Hanseatic   95p
4 b.c Galileo (Ire) – Insinuate (USA) (Mr Prospector (USA))
2012 p8m* Nov 8

Insinuate didn't get long to show her worth on the track, her career amounting to just four starts in the space of two months, but she did chalk up a win in listed company and, unsurprisingly for one bred to be a top-notcher (her dam is Prix du Moulin winner All At Sea), she has made a more lasting impact as a broodmare. She has produced five individual winners to date, with very smart Group 3 winner Stronghold and listed race scorer Take The Hint the best of them so far. Both represented the powerful John Gosden/Khalid Abdulla combination, and that duo look to have another smart prospect on their hands in Hanseatic, the latest of Insinuate's progeny to make the course.

Hanseatic has presumably had a problem or two, not making it to the track until the tail end of his three-year-old season, but he quickly went about making up for lost time with an impressive win in a polytrack maiden at Lingfield. Sent off favourite, Hanseatic looked green when first pressured but found plenty once the penny dropped, leading inside the final furlong and looking to have more in hand than the margin of two lengths over runner-up Rockalong suggests. Subsequent events suggest the race was stronger than might be expected for a three-year-old maiden that late in the year—Rockalong won a similar event at Kempton later in the month and the third and fourth have won three races between tham over the winter—and with that in mind the official handicapper looks to have taken a chance with an initial mark of 80 for Hanseatic, especially when factoring in the colt's potential for improvement. Indeed, Hanseatic, who should stay a mile and a quarter, could well be up to making an impact in listed/minor pattern company further down the line. **John Gosden**

Havana Beat (Ire)   91p
3 b.c Teofilo (Ire) – Sweet Home Alabama (Ire) (Desert Prince (Ire))
2012 7.1m^2 8.1m* Sep 19

Former Finance Director of Coral Mick Mariscotti and his wife Janice have been owners with Andrew Balding since 2007 and have seen their white, emerald green hoops, dark blues sleeves and cap carried to success by the likes of Goldoni, Mon

Cadeaux and Zanetto in recent seasons. The couple, whose colours derive from Mick's love of Tottenham Hotspur and Janice's of Glasgow Celtic, are also the owners of useful prospect Havana Beat and we expect their colt to net a handicap or two in 2013.

Havana Beat confirmed the promise of his debut at Sandown (head second to Etijaah, with *Horse To Follow* Hillstar fourth) when winning a ten-runner similar event by two and three quarter lengths at the same course three weeks later. That race, in which favourite Havana Beat stayed on strongly to lead in the final furlong, looked an above-average one of its type at the time, and that opinion was franked when runner-up Restraint of Trade and third Nichols Canyon improved to take maidens on their next outings, the former adding a minor event at Newmarket later in the season for good measure. Havana Beat looked far from the finished article as a juvenile and can be expected to progress further as he gains more experience, and he has plenty of scope to improve physically, too, tall but rather unfurnished as a two-year-old. As a half-brother to two-mile winner King's Realm (by King's Best), Havana Beat will be suited by at least a mile and a quarter as a three-year-old, when he'll be well worth following in handicaps. *Andrew Balding*

Heeraat (Ire) 113
4 b.c Dark Angel (Ire) – Thawrah (Ire) (Green Desert (USA))
2012 6d³ 6m⁶ 5d³ 6m³ 6m⁴ 5d* 6f* 6v⁵ Oct 13

William Haggas is probably most famous for his achievements in the Epsom classics, saddling Shaamit to Derby success in 1996 and Dancing Rain to victory in the Oaks in 2011, but his record with sprinters shouldn't be overlooked. Since the turn of the century Haggas has saddled such notable performers as Prix Maurice de Gheest hero King's Apostle, Flying Childers winner/Abbaye runner-up Superstar Leo and her smart daughter Enticing, and last year's Cheveley Park scorer Rosdhu Queen. In Hamdan Al Maktoum's Heeraat, we believe Haggas has another speedster worth following, one who will take the well-worn path from valuable sprint handicaps to pattern-race success in the new season after progressing to a smart level during an impressive three-year-old campaign.

Heeraat gained reward for a string of solid efforts when narrowly beating Profile Star in a five-furlong apprentice handicap at York in August, digging deep under pressure, and he followed up over six furlongs on very different ground at the same venue in a highly competitive twenty-runner event less than three weeks later. Heeraat justified joint-favouritism when beating Hamza by a neck on the latter occasion, and the form proved strong with third Gabriel's Lad and fourth Jack

Dexter both winning next time out. He was then sent off at just 7/2 to complete the hat-trick when returned to York to take on his elders for the first time in a valuable event, and shaped much better than the result, travelling very strongly in front but paying late on for going too hard, finishing fifth to Regal Parade and leaving the impression he's still well treated from an official mark of 101.

From the family of his owner's Golden Jubilee Stakes winner Malhub, the good-topped Heeraat has all the hallmarks of one who will progress again as a four-year-old, when races such as the Wokingham and Stewards' Cup will presumably be on the agenda before progressing to pattern races later on: he begins 2013 with a profile very similar to the aforementioned King's Apostle, who was placed in both of those top handicaps as a four-year-old before landing the Diadem in the autumn. Heeraat is versatile as regards underfoot conditions, a winner on firm and good to soft going, and shaping well for a long way on heavy on his final start last term. *William Haggas*

Hillstar   97p
3 b.c Danehill Dancer (Ire) – Crystal Star (Mark of Esteem (Ire))
2012 7.1m⁴ 7s* Oct 16

If television interviews are to be believed there are few things that can put a smile on Ryan Moore's face. However, surprisingly enough, a trip to Leicester may be one of them as over the past five seasons the former champion has enjoyed a profit of £13.92 to a £1 level stake at the track. One contributor to that tally was Hillstar, who improved significant from his promising debut when justifying 2/1 favouritism in a maiden there last October. The manner in which Hillstar, who carries the dark blue, yellow cap of British financier Sir Evelyn de Rothschild, put his eleven rivals to the sword that day suggested he's a colt of real potential. Having travelled powerfully, Hillstar responded well to his rider's urgings and always looked as if he was going to reel in the leader, surging to the front late on and appearing to have plenty left in his locker as he passed the post three quarters of a length in front of runner-up Flashlight. A sturdy half-brother to the yard's Crystal Capella, who was a multiple pattern-race winner at up to a mile and a half, Hillstar looks sure to progress as he gains experience, with trips in excess of a mile likely to play to his strengths. Considering his Timeform rating, Hillstar's initial handicap mark of 83 looks extremely lenient, though a Derby entry suggests connections may harbour loftier ambitions. Either way, he could hardly be in better hands, with Sir Michael Stoute a past master at conjuring steady improvement out of unexposed three-year-olds. *Sir Michael Stoute*

Huntsmans Close   92p
3 b.g Elusive Quality (USA) – Badminton (Zieten (USA))
2012 7s² 6g 6m² 6g² 6v* Oct 23

In a relatively quiet year for Jamie Spencer, in which Wigmore Hall's success in Canada provided his only win at the top level, his dead-heating for first place in the fiercely competitive season-long 'Six to Follow' challenge on Michael Bell's website was presumably up there with his biggest achievements. More shrewd selections are required if he wants to make a successful defence of his crown in 2013, however, and it would be no surprise were Huntsmans Close, a highly promising sprinter who Spencer rode four times last year, the first name on the team sheet.

It may have taken a while for Huntsmans Close to get to grips with what was required under pressure, but his abundant potential was clear from the outset. Even before a most encouraging debut at Yarmouth, his position as joint favourite up against representatives of other strong stables gave a good indication of the regard in which he was held. In the event, Huntsmans Close faltered into second close home, burning the fingers of in-running punters (traded at 1.01), but it was what went before that caught the eye, making up ground smoothly from off the steady pace and looking in control when taking over before the furlong pole. Exuberance got the better of him on his next two starts, pulling hard when favourite at Goodwood and seeming to have things sewn up at Haydock before producing an underwhelming finishing effort, but any doubts about his attitude were cast aside back at Yarmouth on his final two outings, first making subsequent Racing Post Trophy runner-up Van Der Neer work hard for his winning debut, then getting off the mark in taking fashion under Hayley Turner when forging clear of another subsequent winner in Maid A Million. A well-bred sort (dam was placed in the Lowther and the Cheveley Park Stakes) who is likely to have filled out over the winter—a gelding operation will also have helped him to settle down—it's not difficult to imagine the strong-travelling Huntsmans Close ending up in listed company, probably over sprint trips for all that he stays seven furlongs. He therefore looks favourably treated heading into handicaps off a BHA mark of 86.
Michael Bell

Improvisation   96p
3 b.c Teofilo (Ire) – Dance Troupe (Rainbow Quest (USA))
2012 7s² 7g³ Aug 4

PPPPP . . . 'What's all with the Ps?' we hear you cry. Surely an out-of-sorts chaser, pulled up in its last five starts, hasn't somehow snuck into *Timeform's Flat Horses*

To Follow? No, we are instead referring to the 'five Ps' acronym: Proper Planning Prevents Poor Performance, though if you are now expecting us to start talking about its relevance to racing, you need not worry. For a start, it's the kind of cringe-worthy saying likely to be uttered by contestants on 'The Apprentice', and secondly, it's not always true. While planning clearly has its place, quick thinking and improvisation can be just as, if not more, important.

After improvising the first part of this piece by tenuously rambling on about improvisation, it appears the time has come to actually talk about its subject. Boasting an attractive pedigree—he is a half-brother to useful Irish winner at up to eleven furlongs Puncher Clynch, out of a mare related to several at least smart performers—Godolphin's useful-looking Improvisation appeals as the sort to step up markedly on what he achieved in a pair of outings last year. On his debut Improvisation kept on well when splitting subsequent big-race winners Ghurair and Dundonnell at Newmarket in a maiden that proved one of the strongest run all year, with plenty of winners further back. He failed to build on that in form terms when only third (beaten a length) to Steeler at Goodwood less than a month later, though neither the track nor the lack of a proper stamina test appeared to suit, and the form of that race hardly looks shabby, either, with the winner going on to win the Royal Lodge. A maiden win is a formality for Improvisation, and it will be disappointing if he doesn't end 2013 with an appreciably higher Timeform rating than he begins the campaign with, with a step up to a mile and beyond sure to suit. *Mahmood Al Zarooni*

Kiwayu 93
4 b.g Medicean – Kibara (Sadler's Wells (USA))
2012 p12g* p12m³ 12.1m⁴ 14.6s³ Oct 26

Horses sold out of Luca Cumani's yard are certainly not the usual starting point when it comes to compiling this list, but Kiwayu was on our radar when still with the Newmarket-based handler, appealing as a handicapper who hasn't yet reached the ceiling of his ability, and a move to the very capable Ian Williams for the not-insignificant amount of 30,000 gns in October certainly hasn't put us off. Williams enjoyed by far his best season to date on the Flat in 2012 when he sent out fifty-seven winners and placed seven horses, including five-time scorers Postscript and Gabrial's King, to win at least three handicaps apiece. Kiwayu is unquestionably in safe hands.

Kiwayu emphatically defied a mark of 69 on his handicap debut at Lingfield in July, beating four next-time-out winners by upwards of six lengths. Despite a 12 lb rise in the weights Kiwayu performed with credit in similar races on each of his three subsequent starts, each time shaping with more encouragement than the bare result, notably when five lengths third of sixteen to Daneking over the extended fourteen furlongs at Doncaster, an eye-catching move three furlongs out taking its toll at the business end. Kiwayu's pedigree—his dam won over an extended eleven furlongs and is a sister to St Leger winner Milan—and the way he shaped over a mile and a half both suggest he'll have no trouble proving himself at the longer trip another day, giving connections plenty of options in the new season, when he's sure to win another handicap or two. The good-topped Kiwayu, who was tongue tied for all his starts last season, acts on polytrack, and his best turf effort came on soft going. *Ian Williams*

Majestic Moon (Ire) 86p
3 b.g Majestic Missile (Ire) – Gala Style (Ire) (Elnadim (USA))
2012 6g² 6g* 6g⁴ 6v Sep 21

Majestic Moon probably won't scale the same heights as his stablemate and brother Majestic Myles, a dual listed winner who has also been placed in pattern races, but he's a promising sort in his own right and well worth following in handicaps this season. Majestic Myles, who is effective at six and seven furlongs, was much improved when winning a valuable handicap off a mark of 93 on his first start in his second season, and Majestic Moon starts 2013 off just 77, with the impression being that his two-year-old campaign failed to get to the bottom of him. After shaping well when second in a maiden at Ayr first time out, Majestic Moon won a similar event at the same track in July by five lengths from next-time-out winner Kolonel Kirkup. More improvement looked on the cards but neither of his two runs in nurseries after showed Majestic Moon to best effect. Sent off at 7/2 in a field of fourteen at York three weeks later, Majestic Moon looked unlucky not to finish much closer having reared leaving the stalls, staying on into fourth behind stablemate Mary's Daughter; and a down-the-field effort as favourite at Ayr on his final start can be put down to the very testing ground, weakening quickly after failing to settle. The promise of that York run in particular suggests Majestic Moon will start the new campaign well treated, and he has obvious potential beyond that given his profile. He's raced only at six furlongs so far but should stay seven. *Richard Fahey*

Mallory Heights (Ire) 75p
3 b.c Dalakhani (Ire) – My Dark Rosaleen (Sadler's Wells (USA))
2012 8.3s p8.6g p8f^2 Dec 12

Craig Bennett sold his shareholding in the parent company of a leading mobile phone retailer for a whopping £73m in 2006 and soon set about fulfilling a lifelong dream of laying the foundations of a breeding operation that would stand the test of time. As part of a £7m broodmare-buying spree designed to firmly establish his newly formed Merry Fox Stud, Cheshire-based Bennett shelled out 2.5m gns on a Sadler's Wells yearling out of the blue-blooded Brigid in 2007, a record for a filly sold in Europe that year. While Liffey Dancer failed to even make the track, Merry Fox have produced Mallory Heights from a mare they purchased from Ballydoyle for a much lesser sum (190,000 gns) a few years ago and he looks a colt with a bright future having shown highly progressive form in three maidens as a two-year-old.

Mallory Heights, who runs in the colours made famous by the likes of Purple Moon and Noble Alan in recent seasons, was backed into 8/1 at Kempton on his final start having shaped with a degree of promise amid greenness previously. In the hands of stable apprentice Patrick Hills, Mallory Heights caught our eye as he stayed on well from mid-field to finish second, beaten under two lengths by favourite Ningara. It was a performance that suggests there'll be plenty of improvement from Mallory Heights in handicaps in 2013, when he seems sure to be suited by at least a mile and a quarter: he's by Arc winner Dalakhani and his dam, who was placed over an extended nine furlongs, is from the family of French Derby (when that race was run over a mile and a half) winner Sanglamore. *Luca Cumani*

Mean It (Ire) 91p
4 b.g Danehill Dancer (Ire) – Lilissa (Ire) (Doyoun)
2012 8d^2 8g* Jul 20

Despite saddling the winner of the Royal Hunt Cup in Prince of Johanne, 2012 will not be remembered too fondly by Tom Tate as he sent out just one other winner during the Flat turf season. He also lost the patronage of his most high-profile supporters in Dr Jim and Fitri Hay, and consequently the promising Mean It, who provided Tate with that other success. In 2013 Mean It will race for David Simcock, who conversely had his best season so far with sixty-eight winners during the calendar year.

Mean It is well bred, as a brother to mile winner Saturn Girl and a half-brother to several at least useful winners, including the smart Irish mile and a quarter winner Livadiya, so it is no surprise that he fetched as much as he did (€200,000) as a yearling. A 7/2-shot for a seven-runner maiden at Haydock on his belated debut in mid-June, Mean It failed by three quarters of a length to catch the fairly useful Kaafel, who later won a handicap off a mark of 82, but he still looked an above-average prospect in pulling sixteen lengths clear of the remainder. Four weeks later Mean It didn't need to improve to land the odds in a twelve-runner similar event at the same course by three and a half lengths from next-time-out winner Sunnybridge Boy. Having travelled strongly, Mean It took it up over a furlong out and had plenty in hand come the line, the performance again suggesting there is a good deal of improvement to come further down the line.

While the fact that he was unraced at two and not seen after July last year is a slight concern, there's little doubt Mean It is going to prove better than an initial BHA mark of 77, probably by a fair way granted a clear run, and therefore very much one to keep on side in handicaps. Though his pedigree suggests he may stay further, two strong-travelling efforts over a mile suggest that trip is fine for him at present. *David Simcock*

Mystery Bet (Ire) 88p
3 b.f Kheleyf (USA) – Dancing Prize (Ire) (Sadler's Wells (USA))
2012 6m³ 7v* Oct 13

Ladys First improved significantly in 2012 and contributed a small profit to this publication's final balance sheet owing to her win in a listed race at Haydock. While it remains to be seen whether she can land a black-type contest of her own, we fancy another Helen and Norman Steel-owned/Richard Fahey-trained three-year-old filly to prove a progressive money-spinner this season in the shape of Mystery Bet.

Despite finding the trip barely enough of a test, Mystery Bet produced a promising first effort when third of ten—beaten two short heads—to Red Turban in a maiden at Haydock, two and a half lengths ahead of next-time-out winner Valais Girl. Five weeks later, upped in trip in a seven-runner similar race at York, Mystery Bet duly stepped up as expected to get off the mark, finishing strongly to collar Lancelot du Lac deep inside the final furlong, with favourite You Da One back in third. It was a maiden that looked likely to prove strong form despite the relatively small field, with the front three all striking as above average and deserving credit for pulling so far clear of the remainder. Mystery Bet's win in very testing ground suggested that she takes more after her dam, who stayed a mile and a half, than her Jersey Stakes-winning sire in terms of trip requirements, and a step up to a mile promises to suit her well in 2013. This point is further backed up by the exploits of her siblings, including mile-and-a-quarter scorer Firebet, who himself proved a real money-spinner for the Steel/Fahey combination a couple of seasons back. *Richard Fahey*

Nabucco ★ 100p
4 b.c Dansili – Cape Verdi (Ire) (Caerleon (USA))
2012 10g⁴ 10s² 10d* 10s Jul 12

John Gosden is very much a go-to man for many when it comes to older handicappers and a cursory glance at the cold, hard figures confirms why, as at the time of writing the trainer's horses aged four and over have won forty races (at a 21% strike rate) over the last five seasons, yielding a £79.94 profit to a £1 level stake. Royal Ascot winner Gatewood, one of the shining lights among last year's *Fifty*, was a good example of Gosden's skill at placing progressive types and we have high hopes for a similar sort in the regally-bred Nabucco, a son of Godolphin's 1000 Guineas winner Cape Verdi.

Gatewood, who won four races in 2012, went into his four-year-old campaign rated 95p and Nabucco himself has shown a useful level of form after just a handful of races. Second in a very strong maiden at Sandown—aside from winner Signed Up and Nabucco eight of the twelve other runners won before the season was out—on his second start, Nabucco went on to win a similar race at Windsor in June by two lengths from Guarantee, who showed smart form in winning his next three races before being sent off at 12/1 for the St Leger. Nabucco may have run below expectations when only tenth (as favourite) in a three-year-old handicap (off what looked a fair-looking opening BHA mark of 88) at Newmarket on his only subsequent outing but we believe that is best excused, not ideally placed having been patiently ridden and considerately handled once his chance had gone. Forgiving a single disappointing run can often pay dividends, especially when the horse in question has strong previous form to its name, and it is a policy we expect will prove particularly rewarding with Nabucco in the coming season, when he could well end up making his mark in some of the high-end middle-distance handicaps. A sturdy colt who will stay a mile and a half, Nabucco has raced only on good ground or softer. *John Gosden*

 Follow us on Twitter @Timeform1948

David Johnson, Flat Editor (Nabucco): *"John Gosden doesn't persevere with older horses without good reason and there's no doubt Nabucco has unfinished business about him. The form he showed in maidens was notably strong, and he had a number of potential excuses when returning a beaten favourite in what is traditionally a strong handicap at Newmarket's July meeting. Nabucco should be placed to advantage in valuable handicaps, perhaps starting with the City And Surburban at Epsom's Trial meeting, and he could even end up better than that by the end of the year."*

Nine Realms   102p
4 b.c Green Desert (USA) – Bourbonella (Rainbow Quest (USA))
2012 7d² p8m² 8.3m* May 28

March tends to be dominated by one thing in the racing world, namely the Cheltenham Festival. However, if there's one other topic of discussion that's likely to get a look in it might well be 'What's Haggas' Lincoln horse?' Nine Realms has clearly had problems having not been seen since last summer, but the form and promise he'd shown in three maidens had put him firmly on our radar, and that he is one of only two of the trainer's entries for the first major handicap of the season (which Haggas has won three times) and is currently as low as 10/1 are big positives. He looks a colt to keep firmly on side in 2013.

Like Haggas' last Lincoln winner Penitent, Nine Realms didn't run as a two-year-old but quickly progressed into a useful performer at three. An attractive and well-bred sort—he's closely related to the yard's Group 1 mile winner Aqlaam (by Oasis Dream) and a half-brother to fifteen-furlong winner Curacao (by Sakhee)—Nine Realms showed abundant promise in the hands of Liam Jones on each of his runs, finding only the very smart Cogito too good on his debut at Newmarket and then runner-up to Sir Michael Stoute's useful Mawasem at Kempton. Nine Realms stepped up a notch when he slammed useful next-time-out winner Razorbill by five lengths in a thirteen-runner event at Leicester, making all, and considering the strength of his form an opening BHA mark of 93 looks lenient. What's more, he is in the right hands to improve further this term, his trainer having saddled the likes of High Standing, Green Destiny and, of course, Penitent to win big handicaps as four-year-olds in recent campaigns. Nine Realms appeals to us as well placed to emerge as a leading player for the top handicaps over a mile to a mile and a quarter in the new season, quite possibly beginning at Doncaster on March 23. *William Haggas*

Pallasator ★ 108p

4 b.g Motivator – Ela Athena (Ezzoud (Ire))
2012 10m* p12g* 14s* Sep 28

Sir Mark Prescott hasn't managed to win York's Ebor since landing the race with market leader Hasten To Add in 1994, although to be fair he has saddled only five runners in the subsequent eighteen renewals and two of those did make the frame, namely Foreign Affairs (beaten just half a length in 2001) and Motivado. The latter couldn't quite get the job done last year, beaten two lengths into fourth by Willing Foe, but Prescott may not have to wait much longer for a second success in Europe's most valuable Flat handicap as Pallasator looks just the type to land a major staying event this term.

Pallasator doesn't quite fit the typical mould of one from his yard in that he needed only one run before getting off the mark. Already gelded prior to a most encouraging outing as a juvenile, Pallasator returned with a narrow victory over Sound Hearts in a small-field maiden at Leicester in late-July, a useful performance that suggested he would be very interesting in handicaps, especially when upped in trip. Rather generously handed a mark of 85 by the official assessor— Sound Hearts had won a handicap off the same figure in the interim—Pallasator duly landed a mile-and-a-half event at Kempton in the first week of September before rounding off his first full campaign with victory off a 6 lb higher mark at Haydock. Pallasator's performance at Haydock, where he again went in snatches held up before staying on strongly to lead inside the final furlong, was all the more notable for the fact that despite idling close home he beat the now useful Nicholascopernicus comfortably while conceding 7 lb.

Despite an unbeaten campaign, Pallasator still looked rather raw at times, both before (tended to sweat and become edgy in the preliminaries) and during his races, suggesting more to come as he matures; and he physically appeals as the type who will thrive with another winter under his belt, too, given his huge frame. It's all positive at present with Pallasator, and we fully expect him to be a major player in the big staying handicaps in 2013, with his trainer already likely to have an eye on York's big prize. He acts on polytrack, soft and good to firm going. *Sir Mark Prescott*

Pearl Secret   119p

4 ch.c Compton Place – Our Little Secret (Ire) (Rossini (USA))
2012 5s* 5g* 5s* 5g Aug 24

David Barron has long been saying that Pearl Secret is the fastest horse he has ever saddled, which is high praise indeed from a vastly-experienced trainer who has been responsible for the likes of Nunthorpe winner Coastal Bluff and, more recently, July Cup third Hitchens. While it is true that Pearl Secret did fail to live up to expectations when faced with his first big test last term, he had already gone a long way to vindicating Barron's opinion of him and looks the sort who will very much come into his own as a four-year-old. In short, his inclusion as a member of our *Fifty* for the second successive year needs little justification.

Pearl Secret will make his mark in the top sprints this year

The Nunthorpe was the race in which Pearl Secret, the winner of a handicap in April, a minor event in May and a listed race in June, met with his sole defeat, and it's one which is easily excused. Behind only the joint-favourites in the betting despite taking a big step up in class and racing outside of his own age-group for the first time, Pearl Secret had just about the worst of the draw as things turned out and had little go right in the race, poorly placed having been waited with then hampered when trying to improve over a furlong out. In the circumstances he did well to be beaten only four lengths in finishing ninth behind Ortensia, and we remain with the firm belief that he can strike at the highest level.

As was pointed out in this publication last year, Pearl Secret's pedigree is pure speed, which he'd shown plenty of in his three wins prior to York, travelling strongly each time. A sprinter on looks, too, the strongly-built Pearl Secret has been kept to five furlongs so far and, in view of his free-going nature, it could be that it proves his optimum trip (though he should stay six furlongs if he learns to settle). Pearl Secret acts on soft going and has yet to race on firmer than good. *David Barron*

Plutocracy (Ire)   65p
3 b.c Dansili – Private Life (Fr) (Bering)
2012 7g 8.3s⁶ p7g Nov 1

Plutocracy means rule by the wealthy, and Bjorn Nielsen, the American-based hedge-fund partner, certainly isn't short of a bob or two judging by some of his acquisitions at the sales in recent years. A combined 810,000 gns bought him a St Leger winner and a third in Masked Marvel and Michelangelo, while the 150,000 gns he paid for another member of our *Fifty*, last season's highly progressive stayer Biographer, looks a good investment now. However, the owner is also a keen breeder, and his pairing of Dansili with Private Life, a useful French eleven-furlong winner purchased from Daniel Wildenstein for 70,000 gns in 2006, looks to have produced a horse capable of climbing the ranks in handicaps this term.

Plutocracy showed only modest form in three races as a juvenile but his progressive performances promised better to come, with his final effort suggesting that his future lies over at least a mile. Sent off a 25/1 chance for a ten-runner maiden at Lingfield on that occasion, Plutocracy was momentarily outpaced in rear before staying on to finish a never-nearer seventh to the Sir Michael Stoute-trained debutant Chengho. Once again in the hands of stable jockey Ted Durcan, Plutocracy shaped like a colt who could prove a fair bit better than his opening mark of 70. In an interview last year Nielsen confessed that he has 'been known to have a good wager', and it would be no surprise to see the money come for Plutocracy on his handicap bow: his trainers record with three-year-olds in handicaps currently stands at a very respectable 20%. *David Lanigan*

Rivellino 89p
3 b.c Invincible Spirit (Ire) – Brazilian Bride (Ire) (Pivotal)
2012 6m³ 5v p6f* Nov 28

Roberto Rivellino, the Brazilian footballer of the 1960s and '70s, is sometimes credited with scoring the fastest goal in history as, during a league match for Corinthians, he netted direct from the kick-off after noticing the opposition goalkeeper on his knees finishing off his pre-match prayers. Connections of the equine Rivellino were most probably expecting a similarly impressive start from their charge on his debut at Ascot in July as he started favourite to beat eleven fellow newcomers, though in the event he had to settle for third in a race won by subsequent Mill Reef hero Moohaajim. While Rivellino blotted his copybook the next two times he was seen on a racecourse—withdrawn at the start when a short-priced favourite at York then producing only a short-lived effort in a heavy-ground listed race at Ayr—such was the impression he had created first time up it was no surprise to see him score easily back in maiden company on polytrack at Kempton following a two-month break. Again well backed, Rivellino proved much too good for his nine rivals, travelling strongly and scoring readily after leading a furlong out. Rivellino, who cost connections 57,000 gns at the Craven Breeze-Up Sales last April, is bred for speed, by Haydock Sprint Cup winner Invincible Spirit and out of a Group 3-winning juvenile sprinter, and we'll be disappointed if he doesn't prove a valuable member of our team this season, when he can strike in a good sprint handicap. *Elaine Burke*

Roanne (USA) 69p
3 b.f Lemon Drop Kid (USA) – Chalamont (Ire) (Kris)
2012 6m 7d⁴ 8d Oct 26

'Makes plenty of appeal on paper and certainly looks the part' was the comment of our racecourse reporter when Roanne made her debut in a maiden at Haydock in early-September. The filly didn't do much to justify a positive report that day admittedly, though held back by inexperience, but her two subsequent runs were more encouraging, and her overall profile bears all the hallmarks of one who will make a much better three-year-old.

On the face of it, Roanne's initial BHA rating (67) is only fair when considering her modest form in maidens as a two-year-old—her fourth of twelve to Alta Lilea at Leicester her best effort—but she left the distinct impression that she could prove a different proposition in time. She's an attractive-looking filly with an abundance of scope for starters, suggesting she'll make plenty of physical development, and her pedigree is hardly shabby, either. Roanne is a half-sister to several winners, including useful seven-furlong/mile winner Secret Garden, and her dam is out of Cheveley Park winner Durtal from the family of Gold Cup winner Gildoran and Arc winner Detroit, all of which contributed to her hefty price tag (150,000 gns). Her prospects are further enhanced by her trainer, who over the last handful of seasons has saddled the likes of three-year-olds Chokurei, Apollo d'Negro, Millyluvstobouggie and Perfect Class to win ten lower-level handicaps between them. All the signs point to a progressive and profitable campaign in handicaps for Roanne as a three-year-old, when she should stay a mile. **Clive Cox**

Robot Boy (Ire) 73p
3 ch.c Shamardal (USA) – Pivotal's Princess (Ire) (Pivotal)
2012 5m 5.1d³ Oct 3

At 115,000 gns Robot Boy was the top lot at the Guineas Breeze-Up Sale at Tattersalls last May when knocked down to David Redvers on behalf of Qatar Racing Limited. While it would be highly optimistic to think that he can repay that outlay in the near future, Robot Boy does look a colt with a bright career ahead of him. David Barron has handled Pearl Secret with typical aplomb, and it is envisaged that he can do the same with Robot Boy in 2013.

Sent off 3/1 second favourite for a maiden at Pontefract in the hands of Frankie Dettori on his debut, Robot Boy was plainly held back by inexperience, but he showed much more on his only subsequent start. This time ridden by Harry Bentley (who will ride as second jockey to Sheikh Fahad in 2013) and after six weeks off, 7/2-shot Robot Boy shaped well in finishing a length and a quarter third of fifteen to Senator Bong in a race that produced no less than five next-time-out winners, motoring home in the closing stages having found the test barely adequate (scrubbed along in the first part of the race). The strong Robot Boy may be out of a useful five-furlong winner (who won her first four starts as a three-year-old), but he looks to have inherited a bit of stamina from his sire and will be suited by at least six furlongs. That Robot Boy was well backed for both his outings suggests he's well regarded by his shrewd yard, and even if he fails to pick up a maiden Robot Boy will still be very much one to have on side in handicaps: his trainer currently shows a level-stakes profit with his three-year-old runners in such races during the last five years. **David Barron**

Royal Dutch $\qquad$ 83p

4 ch.g Nayef (USA) – Shersha (Ire) (Priolo (USA))
2012 7.1s p7f 10s³ p10g* 10m⁵ p11f³ Oct 10

In the 1980s County Cork-born Denis Coakley plied his trade as a National Hunt jockey, wasting little time in losing his claim after joining Gordon Richards as a conditional before spending three years with champion jumps trainer in the States, Janet Elliot. However, since taking out a training licence in 1999 the number of runners Coakley has had over obstacles can be counted on one hand, preferring instead to concentrate on the Flat, with his highest total of winners the fourteen he saddled in 2005. The last two years haven't been bad for Coakley either, with a total of twenty-two winners recorded, and in Royal Dutch he has a progressive handicapper who we expect to make a good contribution in 2013.

After showing promise in maidens, and when third at Newmarket on his handicap debut, Royal Dutch got off the mark in impressive fashion in a similar event on Lingfield's polytrack in August, quickening clear to score by four lengths. A 9 lb rise duly followed and Royal Dutch went on to shape well on both his subsequent outings, especially when third at Kempton on his final start. Again in the hands of Eddie Ahern, Royal Dutch travelled smoothly held up and finished strongly having been left with a lot to do, looking to pass the post with running left in him. There is little doubt that Royal Dutch can win another handicap from his current mark, but he also has potential for ongoing progress beyond that, quite lightly raced for a four-year-old and out of a useful mare who didn't reach her peak until aged five. The rangy Dutch Art looked to appreciate the step up to eleven furlongs at Kempton and seems sure to stay a mile and a half. His best efforts so far have come on polytrack but it's too early to suggest he's not as effective on turf. *Denis Coakley*

Russian Realm ★ $\qquad$ 86p

3 b.c Dansili – Russian Rhythm (USA) (Kingmambo (USA))
2012 8.1g³ Sep 14

Winners of the 1000 Guineas have a mixed record as broodmares and, with the exception of Kazzia (dam of at least smart pair Eastern Anthem and Zeitoper), and possibly Virginia Waters (dam of the useful Emperor Claudius), this century's scorers have so far failed to produce anything of comparable quality to themselves. That said, Russian Rhythm's second foal Safina did manage to finish fourth in the Nell Gwyn as a maiden, and her three-year-old colt Russian Realm may soon prove the pick of her four offerings so far as his sole start as a two-year-old was full of promise.

Owned and bred by Cheveley Park Stud, Russian Realm was the subject of upbeat homework reports prior his debut in a thirteen-runner maiden at Sandown, for which he was sent off joint second-favourite at 6/1. Restrained early by James Doyle, Russian Realm travelled fluently held up until making his effort over a furlong from home, staying on in eye-catching fashion under a hands-and-heels ride to finish two and a half lengths third to market leader Flying Officer. In what looked a strong race of its type on paper—the form was bolstered when fourth Empiricist took a nursery off a mark of 76 on his next outing—Russian Realm joined the winner in marking himself down as an excellent prospect. Incidentally, Russian Realm ran to a figure just 4 lb shy of the one posted by his more precocious dam on her first racecourse appearance. Russian Realm is undoubtedly an exciting proposition for this season and beyond, and he should have little trouble landing a maiden before going on to much better things. He's in the Derby, but on pedigree alone isn't sure to stay beyond a mile and a quarter. **_Sir Michael Stoute_**

Rye House (Ire) 104p
4 b.c Dansili – Threefold (USA) (Gulch (USA))
2012 10v⁴ 11.6s* 12g² Jun 27

While Threefold isn't in the same league as Urban Sea, Hasili or Kind when it comes to her exploits as a broodmare, she is certainly doing her owner Philip Newton proud. Rye House, who presumably takes his name from either the plot of 1683 to assassinate King Charles II of England and his brother (and heir to the throne) James, the Duke of York, or the railway station in Hertfordshire, has been set an impressive standard by his immediate family. Closely related to useful performer at up to two miles Ship's Biscuit, Rye House is also a half-brother to smart pair Hi Calypso (would have stayed two miles) and Warringah (stays a mile and three quarters), as well as the useful Jedi and Cops And Robbers. In fact, all six of Threefold's progeny to have made the racecourse have won a race for Sir Michael Stoute, and we believe Rye House is well on track to land a few more in 2013 on the back of a light but progressive three-year-old campaign.

Following two runs as a juvenile and a fourth at Windsor on his reappearance, the useful-looking Rye House made a winning handicap debut off a BHA mark of 75 at the same course in May, rallying to defeat Man of Plenty by a head, the pair some nine lengths clear of the rest. Not only did Rye House display a good attitude that day, the win also suggested that, in keeping with his siblings, Rye House would

stay even further than a mile and a half in time. In his only subsequent run, in a Salisbury handicap that Hi Calypso had won in 2007 and Warringah had been second in the following year, Rye House shaped just as well despite failing by a head to hold off Rule Book, looking to have established a decisive advantage around two furlongs out but seeming to lose focus in front, something which can be put down to residual greenness for now—he's had only five runs after all. The fact he still finished four lengths and more clear of three next-time-out winners bodes very well for his prospects in 2013, when he'll probably be targeted at some high-end handicaps. He's so far raced mostly on good going or softer (acts on soft).
Sir Michael Stoute

Secret Gesture   93p
3 b.f Galileo (Ire) – Shastye (Ire) (Danehill (USA))
2012 7d² 8v* Oct 27

We fancy Secret Gesture to develop into a live Oaks contender

Jim Crowley enjoyed a first pattern-race win in the Godolphin blue when he deputised for a stuck-in-traffic Frankie Dettori on Tawhid in the Horris Hill at Newbury, but had he thirty-five minutes earlier partnered a horse who might give him a first classic success in 2013? Ralph Beckett trained Look Here to cause a 33/1 upset in the Oaks in 2008 and Secret Gesture, currently trading at the same odds for the fillies' showpiece at Epsom, is no forlorn hope having shown plenty of ability in her two races as a juvenile.

The fillies' maiden won by Lady Nouf at Leicester in October looked a good contest at the time and future events confirmed that impression, with the third-placed Desert Image shedding her maiden tag just three days before Secret Gesture did likewise. On heavy ground, Secret Gesture started at 11/8 in a fourteen-runner similar race at Newbury and had little difficulty in justifying her position as market leader. Making the most of her experience, the Newsells Park Stud-owned and -bred filly needed to improve just a little on her debut form to score, keeping going well having led two out to hit the line with two and three quarter lengths to spare over debutante I Say, the field well strung out. It was a performance that pointed to Secret Gesture being deserving of her place in a higher grade.

The close-coupled Secret Gesture has a pedigree that suggests she will revel in the step up to a mile and a quarter and beyond at three years. By the all-conquering Galileo, the sire of last year's Oaks heroine Was, Secret Gesture is the third foal of Danehill mare Shastye, a listed-placed winner at up to thirteen furlongs when trained by John Gosden. The likelihood of Secret Gesture thriving over middle distances becomes even more certain when it's noted that Shastye is a half-sister to Arc winner Sagamix and high-class mile-and-a-half performer Sagacity. Ralph Beckett saddled Look Here and Colima to finish runner-up in the Lingfield Oaks Trial before running in the Oaks and it would be no surprise should Secret Gesture resurface in the same contest this time round. **Ralph Beckett**

Martin Dixon, Chief Reporter (Secret Gesture): *"Having shaped well first time up at Leicester, Secret Gesture really impressed me when going one better at Newbury, with the Oaks immediately springing to mind given her stamina-laden pedigree. Ralph Beckett knows the way from here after his success with a similar type in Look Here back in 2008, and I fancy this filly won't still be 33/1 after reappearing in one of the trials."*

Secretinthepark   91p
3 ch.c Sakhee's Secret – Lark In The Park (Grand Lodge (USA))
2012 7.1g* p7f* Oct 31

It's fair to say the mare Lark In The Park wasn't much cop on the track, getting her head in front only once from twenty-five starts and even then showing barely modest form to defy a mark of 46 in a handicap at Bath. With a race record like that, only a supreme optimist could expect her to enjoy much success as a broodmare. Nevertheless, her owners, Mia Racing, kept the faith, and they have been rewarded with three winners from four foals to have raced, each one a fair bit better on the track than their dam. The pick of them to date has been Dolphin Rock, a standing dish on the northern racing scene in recent seasons, but his status as the family flag-bearer is under threat from his half-brother Secretinthepark, who is already verging on useful after just two starts in an unbeaten juvenile campaign.

Secretinthepark made his debut at Warwick in August and, not unusually for an Ed McMahon-trained youngster, knew exactly what was required, responding well throughout the final furlong to get the better of Godolphin's Darkening. At the time the form looked only a little better than fair, but Darkening's subsequent exploits, winning a Yarmouth nursery off 77 and going close off 6 lb higher in a hotly-contested event at Newmarket, led to a revision of that view, making Secretinthepark look well-in off an opening figure of 79. It was therefore little surprise to see Secretinthepark, who had been withdrawn on a few occasions in the interim owing to soft ground, sent off a well-backed favourite in a nursery at Kempton, and he made no mistake, travelling strongly up with the pace and always holding Dashing David, with the pair two lengths clear of the rest. A 5 lb rise for that success looks on the lenient side, especially with Secretinthepark likely to improve further as a three-year-old, when we confidently expect him to add to his tally in handicaps at seven furlongs and a mile. *Ed McMahon*

So Beloved ★ 103p

3 b.c Dansili – Valencia (Kenmare (Fr))
2012 7g⁴ 8s* 8s⁵ Oct 24

While the unprecedented exploits of Frankel were unquestionably the reason for Prince Khalid Abdulla being handed awards left, right and centre in 2012, the owner had a winner lower down the racing ladder who we believe will waste little time in climbing a fair few rungs this season. 'He's a huge colt and I hope he will improve as he gets older' said Roger Charlton of So Beloved at the tail-end of October and we have to agree with the Derby-winning trainer.

So Beloved came on appreciably for his debut when creating an excellent impression in winning a fifteen-runner maiden at Salisbury in early-October, travelling as well as any until leading in the last half-furlong and beating subsequent Horris Hill winner Tawhid and Greatwood by upwards of a length. It was a performance that marked So Beloved out as a smart prospect, with the well-made colt possessing the size and scope to suggest he'll train on well. Charlton had taken the Houghton Stakes at Newmarket with Proponent in 2006 and would likely have fancied his chances again in that minor event with So Beloved, sent off an 11/10 chance in a five-runner field in which only nursery scorer Hoarding had run to a similar figure. As it turned out, nothing went right for So Beloved on the Rowley Mile—he stumbled at the start, refused to settle and wasn't persevered with by regular jockey James Doyle once held. We have no hesitation overlooking that effort and are confident that So Beloved will do well in 2013, when an opening BHA mark of 88 is likely to significantly underplay his ability.

Although So Beloved has already won over a mile, both his pedigree (brother to useful 2005 two-year-old six-furlong winner Cantabria, and half-brother to several winners, notably smart sprinter Deportivo) and demeanour suggest it's not out of the question that he may yet prove equally as effective, if not better, over seven furlongs. He has raced on good ground or softer so far. *Roger Charlton*

Adam Brookes, Deputy Print Editor (So Beloved): *"One of Timeform founder Phil Bull's most commonly quoted sayings is: "a time may not tell you how good a horse is but it will tell you how bad a horse isn't", and when So Beloved lost his maiden tag he recorded a timefigure that suggests he is at the very least useful and, therefore, well treated off his initial mark. So Beloved is from a family his trainer has had plenty of success with and was one of the first names on this list."*

Space Ship   82p
3 ch.c Galileo (Ire) – Angara (Alzao (USA))
2012 7.1m⁴ 8g³ 8g⁴ Sep 27

While it's unlikely that John Gosden and Lady Rothschild will be able to repeat last year's annus mirabilis this time round, in Space Ship they have a horse who could take off in handicaps in 2013. The form Space Ship has shown to date may be light years away from competing in the elite races his connections have become accustomed to winning, but we believe he can prove a star in his own right. Space Ship stepped up appreciably on his debut effort when showing fairly useful form to finish third of fifteen to Glenard in a maiden at Doncaster in mid-September, fairly rocketing home having taken time to find his stride. It was a performance that suggested he had the ability to win a similar race at the very least. Although it was therefore relatively disappointing that Space Ship could only match that performance when three and a half lengths fourth of nine to Telescope at Newmarket, time will tell that his effort was almost certainly a solid one in a strong race: each of the runners at HQ were given a 'p' by Timeform's reporter and Space Ship was merely unable to quicken as well as those that finished ahead of him having led over a furlong out. A strong colt with a middle-distance pedigree, we envisage Space Ship coming into his own once upped in trip at three years, with handicaps the obvious starting point from an attractive-looking opening mark of 78. *John Gosden*

Squire Osbaldeston (Ire) 80p
3 b.c Mr Greeley (USA) – Kushnarenkovo (Sadler's Wells (USA))
2012 8m³ Aug 17

'Squire' George Osbaldeston was a nineteenth century English sportsman and politician who became particularly famous for his racing abilities, on one occasion covering two hundred miles in eight hours and forty-two minutes aboard twenty-eight different horses at Newmarket! Osbaldeston's desire to accrue wealth earned from bets and competitions was attributed to his single mother's wild and lavish lifestyle, which meant that his, and his three sisters', inheritance was squandered. After gambling debts of around £200,000 eventually forced him to sell his house, he died almost penniless.

If Osbaldeston was around now, while he'd be peeved that he couldn't partake in his beloved fox hunting, he'd also have the opportunity to get rich (again! … hopefully) by backing the horse named in his honour. Squire Osbaldeston is from a family that has served this publication well in recent years. His dam is a close relative of high-class mile-and-a-half winner Sea Moon and a sister to the dam of Derby/Arc hero Workforce, both of whom were horses to follow in their classic year. It is also the immediate family of St Leger/Racing Post Trophy winner Brian Boru. Squire Osbaldeston arrived at the racecourse, specifically in the Newmarket maiden won by Frankel two years before, with a lofty reputation having cost 100,000 gns as a yearling and with entries in the Royal Lodge and the Dewhurst. Amid definite greenness, the 5/1 chance produced a promising effort, making headway two furlongs out and finishing five lengths third of nine to Altruism in what would prove a solid contest, with both second Tarikhi and fourth Cat O'Mountain winning next time out. Considerately handled by Tom Queally that day, Squire Osbaldeston is sure to progress and looks a banker for a similar race before climbing the handicap ladder. *Sir Henry Cecil*

Follow us on Twitter
@Timeform1948

Telescope (Ire) ★ 96P

3 b.c Galileo (Ire) – Velouette (Darshaan)
2012 7f² 8g* Sep 27

Sir Alex Ferguson enjoyed classic success back in 2002 courtesy of Rock of Gibraltar in the 2000 Guineas, and as one of the dozen owners of the exciting Telescope he has good reason to think that another could come his way at Epsom in June. Telescope became the most expensive yearling ever bought by Highclere Thoroughbreds when purchased for 220,000 gns in a private sale (he missed his date at Tattersalls with a temperature) and it looks money well spent following the very positive impression he created as a juvenile. Sir Michael Stoute could not muster a single classic runner last season but his nine Derby runners since 2003 have yielded three wins—North Light and Workforce were both *Horses To Follow*—a second, a third and a fourth, and Telescope looks his standout contender for the Blue Riband this time around, his current odds of 14/1 likely to appear very generous after he has contested one of the Derby trials. Stoute has won the Dante four times since 2001, while Highclere took the race with Bonfire last year, so it would be no surprise to see Telescope confirm his Epsom credentials on the Knavesmire in mid-May.

Some eye-catching home gallops under Ryan Moore meant Telescope came with a big reputation when making his debut in a seventeen-runner maiden at Ascot in September and he only just failed to justify favouritism (beaten a short head by Snow King) despite having been betrayed by his lack of experience, not settling fully held up and running green when asked to make his move two furlongs out. Ridden that day by Richard Mullen, who was deputising for the injured Moore, Telescope appeared sure to progress and looked a certainty for a similar race. Less than three weeks later, in the hands of Richard Hughes, the odds-on Telescope had little trouble taking a nine-runner maiden at Newmarket from Flkaayed, leading over a furlong out and soon quickening clear without having to be asked for anything like maximum effort. It was such a pleasing performance that the Racing Post Trophy came under consideration, though Telescope ultimately missed that race when his trainer decided it was in the horse's best interests to pull up stumps for the year. Telescope's pedigree suggests he'll have no trouble staying a mile and a quarter, and he has good prospects of getting the Derby trip, too—he's by Galileo for starters, out of a Darshaan half-sister to Dubai World Cup winner Moon Ballad, and his brother, Circumstances, won over an extended mile and a quarter for David Wachman in 2012. A good sort, Telescope has the potential to develop into one of the stars of the season. *Sir Michael Stoute*

The Lark   91p
3 ch.f Pivotal – Gull Wing (Ire) (In The Wings)
2012 8.3d⁴ 8d* Oct 26

Maycocks Bay might well have been too keen from time to time and wandered when asked for her finishing effort on occasions, but surely no one could have predicted how the racing careers of her two most notable offspring to date would have ended. Listed-winning stayer Gull Wing refused to race on her final racecourse appearance in 2008 and two years later dual Oaks winner Sariska also decided enough was enough, refusing on consecutive appearances. Gull Wing's first foal, The Lark, gave no indication that she had inherited any negative family traits in two starts last year and must be given the benefit of the doubt as she starts life in handicaps from an attractive-looking BHA mark of 76.

The Lark, who incidentally shares her sire with Sariska, actually showed a willing attitude when losing her maiden tag at just the second time of asking. Again ridden by Hayley Turner and supported into 7/2 favourite following an encouraging debut fourth at Nottingham, The Lark travelled strongly held up before staying on well to land a fifteen-runner event at Doncaster by half a length from Godolphin's Kalispell. The Lark's much improved and near-useful performance came in what looked a good race of its type, containing quite a few well-bred fillies, and it was given further credence by an impressive timefigure. Michael Bell knows The Lark's family well having trained both Gull Wing and Sariska for owner/breeder Lady Bamford, and we expect him to achieve more success with his latest recruit. A lengthy sort, The Lark will be suited by at least a mile and a quarter. *Michael Bell*

Town Mouse   60p
3 ch.g Sakhee (USA) – Megdale (Ire) (Waajib)
2012 9s p8g⁵ p8m⁶ Nov 8

In terms of prestige this publication has done well with horses trained by Hughie Morrison over the last few years. Sagramor landed a brace of valuable handicaps in 2011, including the Britannia, and Shirocco Star improved over 30 lb from the end of her juvenile campaign to the culmination of a three-year-old one which saw her placed in numerous good races, including the Epsom and Irish Oaks. That Shirocco Star failed to get her head in front in 2012 was admittedly disappointing, but it's hoped that stable-companion Town Mouse can make up for it at a lower level in 2013, with the son of Sakhee appealing as the type to make a better three-year-old.

In terms of bare form Town Mouse, part-owned by former trainer Mouse Hamilton-Fairley, doesn't have that much to recommend him, failing to beat a horse home on his debut before producing a couple of modest efforts. However, he offered enough in those two starts over a mile at Lingfield—four and three quarter lengths sixth of nine to Swing Easy on the latter occasion—to suggest he could be very interesting when going handicapping from a modest opening mark. Indeed, backing all Hughie Morrison-trained three-year-olds in handicaps over the last five seasons would have comfortably yielded a profit, with the likes of Nottingham, Southwell and Warwick particularly fruitful hunting grounds. A 15,000-guinea yearling, Town Mouse's pedigree screams stamina, with his most notable sibling, the smart Frank Sonata, effective over as far as two miles, and the sooner he steps up in trip the better. *Hughie Morrison*

War Lord (Ire) 60p
3 b.g Aussie Rules (USA) – Carn Lady (Ire) (Woodman (USA))
2012 8s⁶ 7s 7d⁴ Oct 26

David O'Meara has gone from strength to strength since setting up base at owner Roger Fell's Arthington Barn Stables in 2010, with War Poet, a horse purchased for just £2,200 as an unraced three-year-old Darley cast-off, a typical success story for the yard having landed a pair of handicaps, including Thirsk's Hambleton Cup, in his first year on the track in 2011. The unrelated War Lord may have cost a bit more—he was bought at the breeze-ups by his owners Geoff and Sandra Turnbull for €16,000—but it's anticipated that he too can add to the trainer's burgeoning reputation this season.

War Lord ran to just a model level as a juvenile but he showed enough ability in three quick runs in maidens to believe he can make significant progress now eligible for handicaps. A half-brother to a couple of six/seven-furlong winners, War Lord got better as he gained experience and his fourth to Singersongwriter at Doncaster signing off was an eye-catching effort. Despite being shuffled back after a couple of furlongs and finding himself last with half a mile to run, War Lord travelled noticeably well in the hands of stable jockey Daniel Tudhope and responded pleasingly under hands and heels to finish closer than had looked possible at one stage. It was a performance that suggested War Lord was still learning, and that obviously bodes well for his prospects. War Lord will begin contesting handicaps off a mark of just 58 in 2013, and O'Meara and The Turnbulls certainly have an intriguing prospect to go into battle with. *David O'Meara*

Well Painted (Ire)   102
4 ch.g Excellent Art -Aoife (IRE) (Thatching)
2012 7g* 8d2 7g5 7s 7d Nov 10

Although no stranger to success in the classics (think Shaamit and Dancing Rain), William Haggas is also established nowadays as a dab hand at bringing good horses along slowly. Accordingly, no less than four of this year's *Fifty* are Haggas-trained four-year-olds who we believe are yet to show their full hand on the track, rounding off with Well Painted.

In line with such stable stars as Beaten Up and Green Destiny in recent times, Well Painted didn't run as a two-year-old. However, Well Painted quickly made up for lost time when overcoming signs of inexperience to make a winning debut at Newbury's Lockinge meeting last May; and he followed that up with his best effort to date when runner-up to the now-useful Chapter Seven (who received 5 lb) on his handicap debut (BHA mark of 93) over a mile at Doncaster. Well Painted was unable to build on that form in three subsequent starts but left our race reporters with the impression on each occasion that we had yet to see the best from him: "not clear run at a crucial stage, finished with running left" at Chester, "shaped well, caught the eye by the end, just left with too much to do" at Ascot, and "travelled smoothly, not clear run" back at Doncaster on his final outing, with a "the type to rank higher in 2013" thrown in for good measure.

A rangy sort in good hands, Well Painted looks just the type to do more to make a name for himself in his second season, when he should emerge as a big player in all of the major handicaps over seven furlongs and a mile. He's not in the Lincoln, with the stable seemingly having another of our *Fifty* earmarked for that (see Nine Realms), but he will still have plenty of other valuable targets to aim at given the plethora of good-quality seven-furlong handicaps, perhaps starting with the Victoria Cup at Ascot. He's so far raced only on good ground or softer. *William Haggas*

SECTION

Battle of Marengo   116p
3 b.c Galileo (Ire) – Anna Karenina (Ire) (Green Desert (USA))
2012 7d³ 7d* 8g* 8s* Sep 30

The Battle of Marengo, which was fought in 1800 between the French under Napoleon Bonaparte and Austrian forces near the city of Alessandria in Piedmont, Italy, was one of the most important battles of the Napoleonic wars, sealing the success of Napoleon's Italian campaign and allowing him to set about reforming France according to his own vision. Whilst the Coolmore partners' Battle of Marengo won't have such a profound effect on world events, we do expect him to make his mark in 2013.

One of our hardest tasks at this time of the year is to decide which of the battalion of Ballydoyle juveniles to include in this publication, indeed the much vaunted Mars hasn't made the cut this year (a decision that may come back to haunt us), but Battle of Marengo made such great strides last year that we felt he justified his place. A promising never-nearer third at Leopardstown on his debut, Battle of Marengo was unbeaten thereafter, following up a wide-margin victory in a maiden at Gowran with an impressive win in a listed race back at Leopardstown. Joseph O'Brien had to deal with a slipped saddle in the latter but it mattered not a jot as his charge quickened nicely from the front and was able to be eased close home to account for the subsequent Autumn Stakes winner Trading Leather. The Beresford Stakes at the Curragh was his next port of call and, although it was a below-par renewal, Battle of Marengo still made short work of his three rivals, forging clear from two furlongs out to beat Orgilgo Bay with much more in hand than the official winning margin of three and a half lengths would imply.

A strong travelling sort, Battle of Marengo gives the impression that he will stay a mile and a quarter, something that is backed up by his pedigree (out of a winner at up to an extended nine furlongs), and it will be surprising if he fails to prove himself at the very highest level this year. *Aidan O'Brien*

Big Break   112p
3 b.f Dansili – Fame At Last (USA) (Quest For Fame)
2012 7s³ 7g* 7s* Oct 27

The recently-retired Famous Name was a cracking servant to connections, winning twenty-one times in six seasons of racing, with all bar one of those coming at listed level or higher (a Group 1 win was just about the only thing missing from his CV, though he finished second at the top level five times). He never made it

Big Break could be one of Ireland's leading classic hopes in 2013

into *Horses To Follow*, while his half-sister Zaminast admittedly proved a bit of a disappointment in both the 2011 and 2012 editions, but we are confident Fame At Last's latest offering, Big Break, can repay us handsomely in 2013.

Big Break broke off in a maiden at the Galway Festival, often a good sign with one from the Weld yard given his formidable record at Ballybrit, and duly shaped with abundant promise, her third behind subsequent Group 3 winner Magical Dream not telling the whole story as she got caught in a pocket two furlongs out and finished with running left. Big Break was far more clued up next time when landing the odds in a race containing plenty of well-bred sorts from good yards at Leopardstown, scoring by an eased-down four lengths. It's her final start that clinched her place in this list, though, as she made short work of her rivals, including some useful colts, in the Group 3 Killavullan Stakes at Leopardstown, beating Beyond Thankful by three and three quarter lengths. Granted, Big Break's only serious market rival might have disappointed, but the manner of her success still created a most positive impression, the turn of foot she showed to settle matters marking her out as one potentially right out of the top drawer. Big Break, who has raced only at seven furlongs so far but will stay at least a mile, may even succeed where her brother Famous Name failed by gaining that elusive Group 1 win, with her current best odds of 16/1 for the 1000 Guineas looking very generous. *Dermot Weld*

Cape of Approval (Ire)   103
4 b.g Cape Cross (Ire) – Wyola (USA) (Sadler's Wells (USA))
2012 7s 8d 7s⁶ 8d 6s² 5s* 6s* 5d* Sep 15

Recommending a horse that was thriving when last seen six months ago on the basis that it's going to pick up where it left off is always fraught with a degree of danger, especially when the horse in question is a sprinter, but in landing his final three races in 2011 Cape of Approval impressed to such an extent that he is confidently included in this list. Tried over seven furlongs and a mile on his first four starts—he was unraced at two years—Cape of Approval improved appreciably when dropped to sprint trips, finishing a neck second in a maiden at the Curragh in June, before getting off the mark in a similar race at Tipperary in July. Punters clearly thought an opening handicap mark of 78 underplayed Cape of Approval's ability as he was sent off 5/2 favourite on his handicap debut at Cork, and he lived up to his market billing with a length-and-three-quarter defeat of Angel Bright, looking 'up to completing hat-trick' according to our race reporter. Again sent off favourite, in another handicap back at the Curragh, Cape of Approval proved that opinion correct on his final outing with a neck defeat of First In Command despite drifting left after leading inside the final furlong.

Although by a high-class miler and out of a Sadler's Wells mare, it's not difficult to see why Cape of Approval has flourished since sent sprinting, as he is closely related to the smart 2010 Norfolk and Gimcrack winnner Approve, and out of a half-sister to smart Dubai-based sprinter Alo Pura. Cape of Approval came a long way in a short space of time in his first season, and we envisage that trend continuing in 2013, when some of the more prestigious handicaps may well be on the agenda. He's so far raced only on good ground or softer. *Tommy Stack*

Foxtrot Romeo   114
4 b.c Danehill Dancer (Ire) – Hawala (Ire) (Warning)
2012 8m² 8g⁶ 7g⁵ 7m Sep 15

As mentioned in the article on Ursa Major later in this section, 2012 saw a phenomenal return to the training ranks for former top jump jockey Tommy Carmody. It was Carmody's ability to improve the horses he inherited from UK-based trainers which really caught the eye, with the Irish St Leger winner Royal

Diamond, who progressed rapidly through the ranks after landing a Leopardstown handicap in April off a mark of 80, a shining example. Carmody appears certain to have even more firepower at his disposal this year and it will be very interesting to see if the switch to the Curragh will have a positive effect on Foxtrot Romeo.

A useful juvenile, Foxtrot Romeo returned to action last season with a highly encouraging second to Power in the Irish 2000 Guineas at the Curragh, but failed to build on that in four subsequent outings. There were mitigating circumstances, however, as he possibly made his effort sooner than ideal in the St James's Palace Stakes, wasn't beaten far into fifth when taking on his elders for the first time in the Lennox Stakes at Goodwood and wasn't persevered with having been denied a run over a furlong out in the Park Stakes at Doncaster, having also got loose beforehand.

A lengthy, well-made colt, Foxtrot Romeo is likely to continue to struggle in Group 1s, but should get ample opportunities at a lower level this year—with the retirement of Famous Name, there doesn't appear to be much depth in the older horse division in Ireland. Whilst Foxtrot Romeo proved at the Curragh that a mile is well within his compass, it is worth pointing out that his full brothers, Air Chief Marshal and Misu Bond, both failed to win at further than seven furlongs, and he should prove equally as effective at that distance. Regardless of his optimum trip, we expect Foxtrot Romeo to win a race or two in 2013, ensuring that his trainer's name remains up in lights for a while yet. ***Thomas Carmody***

Galileo Rock (Ire)   100p
3 ch.c Galileo (Ire) – Grecian Bride (Ire) (Groom Dancer (USA))
2012 8s* 8g^5 Oct 13

Michael O'Flynn's silks were carried with distinction in top staying races under both codes last year, with China Rock landing the Punchestown Gold Cup over fences for Mouse Morris and Saddler's Rock making amends for his close third in the Ascot Gold Cup with victory in the Goodwood Cup for John Oxx. Saddler's Rock's three-parts-brother Galileo Rock also carries O'Flynn's red and yellow colours, and appeals as the sort to also make his mark in good company this term.

Apparently not one to keep all his eggs in one basket, O'Flynn sent Galileo Rock to David Wachman, and the €150,000 yearling made his debut in a maiden over a mile at Leopardstown in August. An 8/1-shot, Galileo Rock was deeply impressive in accounting for subsequent nursery winner Hall of Mirrors by seven lengths, outpaced and still no better than eighth of twelve entering the final two furlongs but finishing strongly when the penny dropped to lead a hundred and fifty yards out. Galileo Rock was brought over to Newmarket to contest the Group 3 Autumn Stakes on his only subsequent two-year-old outing, and wasn't disgraced in finishing five and a quarter lengths fifth behind Trading Leather, seeming to find the trip inadequate on less testing ground, again outpaced over two furlongs out but unable to pick up to the same effect. With smart mile-and-a-half winner Allexina another close relation, and the likes of Gamut and Derby winner North Light on the distaff side of the family, it's not just his relationship to Saddler's Rock which suggests Galileo Rock, a Derby entry (British and Irish), will flourish over longer distances as a three-year-old. If all goes well through the winter he can be expected to line up in a classic trial in the spring, though ultimately the Queen's Vase at Royal Ascot could prove more up his street bearing in mind his pedigree. **David Wachman**

Indurain (Ire)   72p
4 b.c Teofilo (Ire) – Mamela (Ger) (Protektor (Ger))
2012 10d p12g 10g Sep 9

Since the turn of the year, cycling has made headlines for all the wrong reasons following Lance Armstrong's confession that he used performance-enhancing drugs during much of his career, causing him to be stripped of his record-breaking seven consecutive Tour de France victories. In comparison, Miguel Indurain may have won 'only' five Tour de France titles between 1991 and 1995, but unlike Armstrong, the Spaniard remains in possession of his accolades despite his own brush with the authorities regarding a banned substance. Indurain was noted as a fine time trialist and Olympic time trial champion at Atlanta in 1996. While the horse of the same name was in no danger of producing any significant speed figures of his own in three starts in maidens during an Olympic summer, he displayed enough ability to suggest he can win races in 2013.

After finishing some way down the field at Leopardstown and Dundalk, the tongue-tied Indurain caught the eye in no uncertain terms when seventh of twenty at the Curragh on his final appearance, travelling well under restraint before keeping on in the closing stages without being subjected to a hard ride. A place ahead of him that day was Brinestine who won his next two starts, including a handicap off a mark of 73, which means Indurain, who cost £110,000 at the breeze-up sales and is the first foal of a mare who won a Group 3 over a mile as a two-year-old, appears handily treated off an opening mark of 68, especially with improvement on the cards. Miguel Indurain racked up his own impressive sequence on the contours of the Pyrenees and the Alps, and there's the possibility that this colt could do something similar now sent handicapping. **Ger Lyons**

Kingsbarns

120p

3 b.c Galileo (Ire) – Beltisaal (Fr) (Belmez)
2012 8s* 8d* Oct 27

Aidan O'Brien's domination of Flat racing in Britain and Ireland shows no sign of abating, with the yard's twelve Group 1 wins in 2012 (he also landed three more abroad) including five classics. Nevertheless, by his own high standards O'Brien had a fairly ordinary year with his juveniles, managing just one two-year-old winner in Britain. That did come at the highest level courtesy of the hugely exciting Kingsbarns, however.

Kingsbarns landing the Racing Post Trophy

Kingsbarns, who takes his name from a village on the eastern coast of Fife, made his debut in a rather low-key maiden at Navan in October, and didn't need to come off the bridle to easily account for some average rivals by seven lengths. If that performance was very much style over substance, the fact that his powerful connections saw fit to supplement him for the Racing Post Trophy at Doncaster a little over two weeks later said plenty for the regard in which he was held. Despite facing three more experienced pattern-race winners, Kingsbarns produced a smooth all-round display to beat Van Der Neer by a comfortable length and three quarters, tracking the pace travelling strongly and immediately in control once produced to lead over a furlong out. While there were still signs of inexperience from Kingsbarns, his performance was still around par with recent standards for Racing Post Trophy winners.

A rangy and attractive colt, Kingsbarns will go on improving. While middle distances will prove within his range, the Derby surely the number one target, Kingsbarns displayed a high cruising speed as a juvenile and it's not hard to see why he's only around 7/1 for the 2000 Guineas. Although his profile will mean that obvious comparisons will be made with his stablemate Camelot, we think Kingsbarns has the potential to establish himself as a major star in his own right this year, when he has good claims of bringing further classic success to Ballydoyle. *Aidan O'Brien*

Montebell (Ire)   106
4 b.f Dylan Thomas (Ire) – Megec Blis (Ire) (Soviet Star (USA))
2012 10s³ 12d* 12.5m² 12g* Sep 9

Ken Condon has seen both sides of the racing coin since taking out a licence to train in 2002. Curragh-based Condon, who spent five years under the tutelage of John Oxx and often wintered Stateside with the likes of Todd Pletcher, saddled three winners in his debut season but had a winnerless 2003. Highs with the likes of stakes-winning juveniles Norman Invader and Porto Marmay in 2007 were once again short lived as 2008 and 2009 bought just three winners between them. Eighteen winners in both 2011 and 2012 suggest Condon is on the cusp of establishing himself fully, however, and in Montebell he has a horse who can take him to the top tracks this season.

Unraced as a two-year-old, Montebell showed useful form in four starts last term. She built on an encouraging debut in a maiden at Navan when landing a similar race at Cork just under a fortnight later, and stepped up again when losing out only to the now smart Hartani (won the Curragh Cup and second in the Irish St Leger Trial on next two starts) in a minor event at Tipperary in May. Despite a four-month absence, Montebell resumed her progress to land a twelve-runner handicap at the Curragh on her final outing by half a length from Placere, idling in front. The fact that Montebell's victory was just workmanlike meant she was raised only 3 lb to an official mark of 95, and she can win another handicap or two before graduating to listed and possibly even minor pattern level. Montebell stays an extended mile and a half and acts on good to firm and good to soft going. *Ken Condon*

Munsaab (Ire)   62p
7 b.g Alhaarth (Ire) – Claustra (Fr) (Green Desert (USA))
2012 12s 7v Oct 16

County Cork-based James Motherway, best known for training 2010 Irish Grand National heroine Bluesea Cracker, may have saddled just one winner on the Flat since sending out his first runner in 2003 but it will be surprising if he doesn't add to that tally in 2013 courtesy of the potentially very well handicapped Munsaab.

Munsaab was purchased on behalf of Hamdan Al Maktoum for €140,000 as a yearling but was picked up by his current trainer for just €9,000 as an unraced two-year-old. Aged four, he made a winning debut in a bumper at Punchestown, and over the course of the next two seasons established himself as a fairly useful handicap hurdler at up to two and a half miles, getting off the mark over timber at Wexford in October 2011 and producing a career-best when second in another big-field contest at Naas during the latest jumps season. Munsaab has shown enough ability in three starts on the level to think he can win races in this sphere too, again not given a hard time when a remote eighth of sixteen to Olympiad at Gowran on his reappearance and simply racing over an inadequate trip at the Curragh on his latest start. As a Timeform 125-rated hurdler Munsaab, a sibling to four Flat winners, looks thrown in off an opening mark of 55 on the level and can ram the point home when returned to at least a mile and a quarter. *James Motherway*

Sinaniya (USA)   89P
3 br.f More Than Ready (USA) – Sindirana (Ire) (Kalanisi (Ire))
2012 7s* Jun 29

With the likes of Azamour, Dalakhani and Sinndar from families cultivated by the Aga Khan it is no surprise that the owner-breeder has to pair outside stallions with a significant proportion of his broodmare band. It hasn't been straight to Galileo and Montjeu for the open-minded owner, however, as in 2012 he had home-bred winners sired by the likes of Bachelor Duke, Dubai Destination and Oratorio, while his shipping of Sinndar's half-sister Sindirana to the States in 2009 in order to be covered by More Than Ready already looks inspired. The product of that pairing, Sinaniya, created a striking impression on her debut when winning a fillies' maiden at the Curragh that featured some well-bred newcomers, and she looks open to considerable improvement. Sent off third-best in the betting at 11/2, Sinaniya made the running and tanked along in the hands of Johnny Murtagh, beating My Special J's by a head, with the margin seeming to underplay her superiority if anything, the winner tiring having had to overcome a slow start to get to the front. Sinaniya didn't make it to the track again in 2012, though in her absence the form was made to look strong, with the runner-up winning a Group 2 two starts later, whilst fourth-placed Hanky Panky finished in the same spot in a listed race and fifth Greek Goddess won a maiden on their next respective outings. Quite simply, Sinaniya looked something out of the ordinary that day and this Irish 1000 Guineas entry can be fast-tracked to pattern races. A half-sister to ten-furlong winner Sindjara, Sinaniya will stay at least a mile herself. *John Oxx*

Slade Power (Ire)   113
4 b.c Dutch Art – Girl Power (Ire) (Key of Luck (USA))
2012 6g* p7f² 6m* 6s* 6s Oct 20

Despite siring a German classic winner in Caspar Netscher, dual Group 1 winner Dutch Art is still waiting to make that big breakthrough as a stallion. That could be addressed this season, however, as the Cheveley Park Stud resident looks to have some good prospects, headed by Slade Power, a sprinter who looks capable of battling for top honours.

A winner on the second of two outings as a juvenile, Slade Power displayed a fine turn of foot to land a handicap at Cork in April on his reappearance, showing the first glimpse of his true potential. Having been outstayed by subsequent Irish 1000 Guineas runner-up and Jersey Stakes winner Ishvana over a furlong further at Dundalk the following month, Slade Power made no mistake dropped back in trip on his next two starts, taking listed races at Haydock in June and Fairyhouse (beat Arctic half a lengths, future Group 1 winner Gordon Lord Byron fourth) in July. Slade Power wasn't seen again until contesting the British Champions Sprint Stakes at Ascot, in which he came up against some of the best sprinters in Europe. Slade Power's SP of 7/1 was a measure of the progress he'd made earlier in the year but, as it turned out, he wasn't seen to best effect having challenged down the centre of the track, not disgraced in finishing four and a half lengths eighth of fifteen to Maarek.

Edward Lynam is still looking to add to his initial Group 1 triumph achieved when Sole Power, unsurprisingly in the same ownership as Slade Power, shrugged off odds of 100/1 to take the 2010 Nunthorpe. However, we fancy Slade Power will be making his presence felt in some of the better sprint races this season, which could well turn out a big year for both his trainer and sire. He acts on polytrack, soft and good to firm ground. *Edward Lynam*

Snakes And Ladders (Ire) 58p

3 br.c Rock of Gibraltar (Ire) – Jalisco (Ire) (Machiavellian (USA))
2012 6v 7v^6 6s Oct 21

'The safest way to double your money is to fold it over once and put it in your pocket'. Those who backed Time of My Life into evens favourite for the sixteen-runner Black Point Handicap at Wexford in May would have had good reason to disregard that cautionary quote after watching the Tommy Stack-trained handicap debutant run out one of the easiest winners of the season in slamming a field of three-year-olds by fifteen lengths, making a mockery of being allotted the lowest handicap mark possible. That was the yard's only runner on the Flat at Wexford in 2012, and, interestingly, the only runner Stack sent there the year before, Whatever It Takes, was gambled into odds-on favouritism for that same handicap over an extended eleven furlongs, albeit managing only third, but winning his next two starts after.

Two successive gambles in the same race. What are the chances of a third? Well, Snakes And Ladders certainly has the profile of one that could be targeted at that contest. Owned, like Whatever It Takes, by J. P. McManus, he goes into his three-year-old campaign completely unexposed after three runs in maidens over an inadequate six and seven furlongs, when hinting at ability under patient rides. He kept on into eighth of twelve behind Francis of Assisi at Naas when last seen, a run which won't have escaped the attention of the assessor, but with luck he'll still be in a position to start off in low-grade handicaps. A Rock of Gibraltar half-brother to a couple of winners abroad, out of useful mile-and-a-quarter winner Jalisco, there is scope for Snakes And Ladders to progress considerably at longer trips this year, whether or not Wexford is the first port of call. *Tommy Stack*

The United States (Ire) 102P

3 ch.c Galileo (Ire) – Beauty Is Truth (Ire) (Pivotal)
2012 7s* Jul 1

Trainers are often said to be creatures of habit, and that certainly appears the case with Aidan O'Brien. Since 2005, he has won the seven-furlong maiden for two-year-old colts and geldings at the Curragh's Irish Derby meeting seven times, with four of those winners going on to score at the highest level. Horatio Nelson, Duke of Marmalade, Rip Van Winkle and Roderic O'Connor are hard acts to follow, but the latest winner of that contest, The United States, has the potential to emulate them.

The United States' margin of victory over Dibayani may have only been a head, but there was an air of inevitability about the result from some way out. Having travelled smoothly in touch, The United States overcame greenness to quicken smartly to lead entering the final furlong and always looked like holding the runner-up thereafter. The fact that The United States was seemingly Joseph O'Brien's choice of three newcomers from Ballydoyle appears an indicator as to the esteem in which he is held. Based on visual impressions alone The United States looked a smart prospect, but in the following weeks the true merit of his performance began to reveal itself, with four of those who finished behind him winning next time, and one, fifth-placed Grafelli, showing smart form when landing a brace of Group 3s.

The United States enters this season with abundant potential, and features in ante-post lists for both the 2000 Guineas (generally 25/1) and Derby (best-priced 25/1), though whether he will stay a mile and a half is questionable, by Galileo but a half-brother to triple Group 3-winning sprinter Fire Lily. Whatever you are doing come this year's Irish Derby meeting, make sure you find the time to watch that maiden, as you may just get a glimpse of the next luminary to emerge from Ballydoyle. *Aidan O'Brien*

Ursa Major (Ire) 118
4 b.c Galileo (Ire) – Inchyre (Shirley Heights)
2012 p10.7g^2 p10.7g* 10s^2 12s* 12s* 14s* 14.6m^4 Sep 15

One of the stories of the 2012 Irish Flat season was the almost Lazarus-like return of Tommy Carmody to the training ranks. Backed by influential owner Andrew Tinkler, Carmody recorded eighteen victories last year, more than he had managed in total during his previous stint between 1993 and 2005, and he even landed a first Group 1 when Royal Diamond narrowly took the Irish St Leger at the Curragh in September. However, while Royal Diamond may be seen as the yard's flagbearer following that success, Ursa Major is actually rated his superior on Timeform ratings and can also prove a shining star for the stable again this season.

Having failed to make the track as a juvenile, Ursa Major quickly made up for lost time as a three-year-old, starting off with a win in a maiden at Dundalk in April, getting up the dying strides to beat subsequent Galway Festival and Irish Cesarewitch winner Voleuse de Couers by a neck. From then on Ursa Major improved in big chunks, finishing second in a minor event at Navan before going to land a hat-trick at the Curragh, namely a pair of handicaps and the Group 3 Irish St Leger Trial in August. Ursa Major defeated Hartani by a length and three quarters

Ursa Major looks just the type to improve again as a 4-y-o

for his first pattern race success, asserting under mainly hands and heels riding after being produced to lead entering the last. Ursa Major ended his campaign by finishing a creditable fourth to Enke in the St Leger at Doncaster (kept on after being outpaced early in the straight), and he looks the type to regain the progressive thread as a four-year-old, when he can make an impact on the Cup scene (likely to stay two miles). The Doncaster run suggests he handles firmish ground well enough, but he clearly goes especially well on soft (has also won on polytrack). ***Thomas Carmody***

Zand (Ire)   97P
3 b.c Zamindar (USA) – Zanara (Ire) (Kahyasi)
2012 8d² 8s* Oct 27

In terms of prestige the Aga Khan's Takar proved a success for this publication in 2012 by winning a Group 3 and a pair of listed races before being transferred to France, and hopefully the same owner's Zand can achieve something similar this season. Zand will surface with a 'Large P' attached to his Timeform master rating having easily won the second of his two starts as a two-year-old, meaning his profile bears an uncanny resemblance to his ex-stablemate's at the same stage in their respective careers.

Zand could well develop into a live Derby contender

With the Frenchman over to partner Hartani in the Irish St Leger later on the card, Zand was ridden by Christophe Lemaire when a very promising staying-on second to Pearl Music in a maiden at the Curragh on his debut. Declan McDonogh, who in November took over from Johnny Murtagh as retained rider for the Aga Khan, was in the plate when Zand landed the odds in an eleven-runner similar event at Leopardstown by three and three quarter lengths from Ghaamer, making all. In just two runs spread six weeks apart Zand had established himself as one of the most promising youngsters in the country. The lengthy Zand is the seventh foal out of the Oxx-trained mile-and-a-half winner Zanara and the fifth to be trained at Currabeg, following the likes of smart twelve-furlong winner Zanughan and the useful thirteen-furlong scorer Zanderi. Irish 2000 Guineas and Irish Derby entry Zand will stay further than a mile—'He should be a nice horse over a trip next season and will start off in the usual races, maybe the Ballysax Stakes' said his trainer—and he is certainly a smart prospect. **John Oxx**

Follow us on Twitter
@Timeform1948

SECTION

THE BIG-NAME INTERVIEWS

Godolphin

Last year saw a return to the top of the tree for Godolphin as their one hundred and forty-nine winners and over £3m in total prize money in Britain meant the boys in blue were crowned champion owner for the eighth time. There was plenty of international success too, with their two hundred and fourteen winners worldwide—one hundred and forty-five of their three hundred and forty-eight horses won—including fifty-nine stakes wins and registering well over $25m in prize money. Last year's sixteen Group 1 winners was a notable achievement also, bettered only once (eighteen in 1999) since Godolphin sent out their first winner on Christmas Eve, 1992. Simon Crisford, the team's racing manager, has kindly discussed with us some of their leading hopes for the new season...

Saeed bin Suroor & Mahmood Al Zarooni

Older Horses

Aesop's Fables (USA) (120) 4 b.c Distorted Humor (USA) – Abhisheka (Ire) (Sadler's Wells (USA)) 2012 5.5g³ 7g³ 8g* 10g² :: 9g⁴ Jan 31 His return in a nine-furlong Group 2 at Meydan on January 31 was promising, as he had a penalty for winning a pretty substandard Group 1 last year. Once he can shake that off life is going to become a lot easier for him; he can't win carrying penalties as he just doesn't have enough class. I would say ten furlongs is very much as far as he wants to go and a mile, a mile and one would suit him fine. He's a good horse, but he's not an elite horse, and to catch him right, number one: his penalty needs to have expired, and number two: you need to then be looking at Group 2 and Group 3s. That's the type of ponds I expect him to be swimming in. *Saeed bin Suroor*

Colour Vision edging out Opinion Poll in the Gold Cup

Colour Vision (Fr) (123) 5 gr.g Rainbow Quest (USA) – Give Me Five (Ger) (Monsun (Ger)) 2012 p16m* 20d* 16g³ 18g 20v³ 16s Oct 20 The Gold Cup is again his main aim. We were a bit frustrated with him last year because when he won the Gold Cup he obviously had a very hard race, but he seemed to come out of it alright. Then watching his subsequent races, visually you'd say he was not running as well as he did at Ascot, but I think his official rating didn't really change. He just wasn't finishing his races as strongly and I can think of no other reason than his Group 1 penalty kept finding him out. He'll run in the same races as last year. *Saeed bin Suroor*

Encke (USA) (123) 4 b.c Kingmambo (USA) – Shawanda (Ire) (Sinndar (Ire)) 2012 10d* 12g² 12m³ 14.6m* Sep 15 I think he'll be dropped to a mile and a half for his first run, though we wouldn't be afraid to step back to a mile and a quarter. Obviously, races like the Coronation Cup and the King George will be his sort of targets, and if we went down the ten-furlong route there's the Prince of Wales's and races like that. We won't be going down the Cup route. *Mahmood Al Zarooni*

Energizer (Ger) (114) 4 b.c Monsun (Ger) – Erytheis (USA) (Theatrical) 2012 8.5s² 8g⁴ 10d* 12m⁶ Aug 22 Obviously, he's got a bit to prove after that disappointing run in the Great Voltigeur, but it seemed to me a falsely-run race and he never got into it. He is a nice horse, and I've got no doubt his Ascot win was a good run, so we'll just have to see how he's looking when he starts back. He'll probably return in a nice mile-and-a-quarter race somewhere, and build up from there. We've definitely got high hopes for him, and we need to forget about that bad run at York. *Mahmood Al Zarooni*

Farhh (128) 5 b.h Pivotal – Gonbarda (Ger) (Lando (Ger)) 2012 8s* 10m³ 10d² 8g² 10.4m² 8g² Sep 16 He's had his issues and he's not the most straightforward horse, he does need careful attention, but he was brilliant last year, running well behind Nathaniel in the Eclipse and behind Frankel on a couple of occasions, and we very much hope he can win a Group 1 this season. We might drop him back to a mile in the Lockinge for his first race or we might run him in something like the Brigadier Gerard, we haven't decided yet, but he seems to have done well over the winter. Most of the big races for a horse like him are in the second half of the season, so we don't want to be in too much of a rush early on with him. I can't see him being any better this year, but his form certainly entitles him to be winning races at the highest level. *Saeed bin Suroor*

Hunter's Light (Ire) (118) 5 ch.h Dubawi (Ire) – Portmanteau (Barathea (Ire)) 2012 10.3v⁶ 10g³ 12g 10.4m* a10g* 9.8s² 10d* :: a9.4g* Feb 7 He wintered out in Dubai, where he won the second round of the Al Maktoum Challenge at Meydan on his reappearance. He's going to find life difficult in the big races throughout the rest of the year, however, particularly with his Group 1 penalty. I think he's going to be

Farhh should be up to landing a Group 1 this year

a difficult horse to place as he's not good enough to win the big races in England, so he will again have to go overseas. *Saeed bin Suroor*

Masterstroke (USA) (119) 4 b.c Monsun (Ger) – Melikah (Ire) (Lammtarra (USA)) 2012 11d* 11g² 12d² 12g* 12.5g* 12v³ Oct 7 A mile and a half is his best trip, and he might even run in the Sheema Classic at Meydan on World Cup night (March 30). He's another on that Coronation Cup-King George route. *Mahmood Al Zarooni*

Opinion Poll (Ire) (120) 7 b.h Halling (USA) – Ahead (Shirley Heights) 2012 14g² 16g* 16.4g* 20d² 16s Oct 20 He wasn't right after the race (Long Distance Cup) on Champions' Day at Ascot, but we left him in England, gave him the winter off and he seems to have recovered now. We'll have a look and see how he's shaping up at the end of March, but he is getting on a bit. Unlike last year, he won't run in Dubai. *Mahmood Al Zarooni*

Saint Baudolino (Ire) (121) 4 b.c Pivotal – Alessandria (Sunday Silence (USA)) 2012 a8g² 10d² 9.8s* 9d* 10.5g² 12d³ 10g* :: a9.4g⁴ Feb 7 He shaped well when fourth to Hunter's Light in a Group 2 at Meydan on his return. He's pleasing us enormously at the moment and is an exciting horse. He's pretty much a mile-and-a-quarter performer; I don't think he really stays much further than that. He's at the sort of level for races like the Prince of Wales's. *Mahmood Al Zarooni*

Willing Foe (USA) (113) 6 b.g Dynaformer (USA) – Thunder Kitten (USA) (Storm Cat (USA)) 2012 12m³ 14d* 15.5g³ 12s³ 12v Oct 27 We won't really identify our Melbourne Cup team until mid-summer, but I don't think he is the right horse for that race. He's now in no-man's land as he's not going to be winning handicaps off 107, so we'll be looking at Group 3s, listed and conditions races for him, though generally speaking there will always be something rated a bit higher than him that's better than him in those contests. *Saeed bin Suroor*

Three-Year-Olds

Cat O'Mountain (USA) (95p) 3 b.c Street Cry (Ire) – Thunder Kitten (USA) (Storm Cat (USA)) 2012 8m⁴ p8g* p8f* Oct 24 He stayed in England over the winter. I hope he can translate his polytrack form back on to the turf, though a lot will depend on how he starts off. He's got a nice pedigree—he comes from a good American family – and I would say he's a pretty nice horse, but he'll have to contest high-end handicaps now and will need to pull out a bit more. He won twice at Kempton last year and looked like he loved the surface, which isn't surprising given his sire. *Mahmood Al Zarooni*

Certify (USA) (113) 3 b.f Elusive Quality (USA) – Please Sign In (USA) (Doc's Leader (USA)) 2012 6s* 7m* 8g* 8g* Sep 28 I saw her recently and she looks well; she hasn't grown much but she has filled out a bit and has had a good winter. Whether she'll be our sole representative in the 1000 Guineas we don't know yet, but she's certainly our credible contender. Obviously, she's a Group 1 winner, a multiple group winner, and we're looking forward to seeing her. It's unlikely that she'll have a prep race before Newmarket—she's not the type of filly that needs one. She's a course-and-distance winner (regarding the Guineas), which will stand her in good stead. She stayed in Britain over the winter but my view is that is doesn't make any difference; we've had lots of classic success in the spring with horses who have wintered in Dubai, many more than with horses that haven't, in fact. *Mahmood Al Zarooni*

Dawn Approach (Ire) (126p) 3 ch.c New Approach (Ire) – Hymn of The Dawn (USA) (Phone Trick (USA)) 2012 5d* 6d* 6g* 6g* 7d* 7g* Oct 13 When I last talked to Jim Bolger he was very happy with him, he said he's done very well over the winter. Obviously we'll go for the 2000 Guineas, and then we'll make decisions about where he goes next afterwards, whether it be sticking to a mile for races like the St James's Palace or stepping up to a mile and a quarter or even taking his chance at Epsom. There's got to be a doubt about him staying the Derby trip based on the distaff side of his pedigree and, though he races like a horse that's going to go further than mile, we don't know how much further. *Jim Bolger*

Last season's leading juvenile Dawn Approach

Improvisation (Ire) (96p) 3 b.c Teofilo (Ire) – Dance Troupe (Rainbow Quest (USA)) 2012 7s^2 7g^3 Aug 4 He's a nice horse, there's no doubt about that, but we need to see him win his maiden first. I know he ran a good race at Newmarket, and again when behind Steeler at Goodwood, but he needs to get that victory under his belt before we make any plans. He's another one with an interesting pedigree and I guess he's going to stay pretty well. *Mahmood Al Zarooni*

Secret Number (95P) 3 b.c Raven's Pass (USA) – Mysterial (USA) (Alleged (USA)) 2012 p8f* Oct 24 He's still a little bit on the weak side, but is out in Dubai and could run on March 9. He's only a maiden winner, so has an awful lot to prove before he can be talked about in the same light as some of our others, but if he runs well on his return we'll consider him for the UAE Derby. Otherwise we'll just put him away and bring him back to Europe. Either way, he's got the pedigree (half-brother to the likes of high-class/smart milers Dubai Destination and Librettist) and is a nice horse who will end up going ten furlongs, or even further. *Saeed bin Suroor*

Tamarkuz (USA) (105p) 3 ch.c Speightstown (USA) – Without You Babe (USA) (Lemon Drop Kid (USA)) 2012 7m^4 7.1g^2 p7.1f* p7f* Oct 10 He's another who spent the winter in Britain. He's very much like Cat O'Mountain in that he has to translate his polytrack form back to turf and may find himself in no-man's land if he doesn't step up; he's been raised from 82 to 96 after winning a nursery at Kempton on his final start. If he can just make that little advancement to listed class, that would be good. *Saeed bin Suroor*

Tawhid (113p) 3 gr.c Invincible Spirit (Ire) – Snowdrops (Gulch (USA)) 2012 7f 8s² 8.3v* 7v* Oct 27 Obviously his best form, when he won the Horris Hill, was on heavy ground but he could easily run in the Greenham, and then we'd see about the Guineas. I'm not saying he's dependent on soft ground, but he's clearly better on that ground than he is on quick ground. *Saeed bin Suroor*

Steeler (Ire) (115) 3 ch.c Raven's Pass (USA) – Discreet Brief (Ire) (Darshaan) 2012 7g² 7g* 7m² 7m* 8g* 8d³ Oct 27 He's going very well at the moment, we're very happy with him. Whether he starts in the Guineas or the Dante is a decision that has yet to be made, but he's a possible for Epsom at this early stage (33/1 and not currently entered). His run in the Royal Lodge indicated that he had every right to be considered for races like the Derby, and his Racing Post Trophy performance was also very strong. He had to do it the hard way that day and the way the race was run probably didn't suit him. He looks a very nice individual and I think he's a very interesting horse. He's out of a Darshaan mare, so there's no reason why he shouldn't improve when he goes over a trip, and I don't see any reason why he wouldn't be a very live Derby contender. *Mahmood Al Zarooni*

Marco Botti

Marco Botti is a trainer going places—Arlington, Melbourne and Meydan all featured on his itinerary last year and will most probably do so again this time round. At home, Botti has not long moved across Newmarket and into a new state-of-the-art yard he has named Prestige Place in honour of the Goodwood race in which Sesmen provided him with his first group success in 2006. Botti's first runners from the stable, which encompasses one hundred boxes, a treadmill, an equine swimming pool and a range of other mod-cons, got off to a promising start on the all-weather during the winter and the Italian will be hopeful he can beat last year's career-best fifty-two winners over the course of this campaign. Marco has generously outlined the future prospects of some of his leading performers here…

Older Horses

Fattsota (115) 5 b.g Oasis Dream 129 – Gift of The Night (USA) (Slewpy (USA)) 2012 p11m 9s⁴ 11.6g² 10d⁴ 12m* 12m² 12s* 12v⁶ :: 2013 12.1g Feb 14 He is in Dubai and training well, but unfortunately he doesn't have many races open to him out there—his best trip is a mile and a half, and perhaps he might be better with a little bit of juice in the ground. He didn't run badly when seventh in a handicap at the carnival in February, but probably needs to improve to defy his current mark (107).

Grey Mirage (96) 4 b.g Oasis Dream 129 – Grey Way (USA) 109 (Cozzene (USA)) 2012 p8g* 8.1v* 8d 8g⁵ p9.5g³ p8f⁶ p8f* :: 2013 p8m² Feb 2 He won at Lingfield (first time cheekpieces) in December and will likely have a turf campaign; he handles some cut in the ground. Last year he was gelded and also he had a break, which means he's a lightly-raced horse, so we'll keep him going through the spring and see how he goes.

Guest of Honour (Ire) (97p) 4 b.c Cape Cross (Ire) – Risera (Ire) (Royal Academy (USA)) 2012 p8m⁴ 8s⁵ p8.6g* p8f* Dec 20 He is a horse I like a lot (entered in the Lincoln). He was very backward and had a few niggling problems, which it looks like are now sorted, and I think he could probably progress into a nice handicapper. After he won a class 4 handicap at Kempton in December we just backed off him, and we'll give him a little bit of time. He's doing well, and I think he can prove better than his current handicap mark (85). He's definitely a miler.

Jakkalberry (Ire) (125) 7 b.h Storming Home – Claba di San Jore (Ire) (Barathea (Ire)) 2012 14g³ 12g³ 12g⁵ 13.5g* 12g 16g³ 12f Nov 25 He ran a good race in the Melbourne Cup and the plan is to run in similar races to last year. He'll start in Dubai and, obviously, work through the summer. The Melbourne Cup will be the priority, so we'll have to work backwards from that after Dubai and see which races we will go for. The plan is to keep him fresh and well for Flemington.

Marcret (Ity) (114) 6 b.g Martino Alonso (Ire) – Love Secret (USA) (Secreto (USA)) 2012 9g³ 8g⁶ 10g⁵ 10.3v* 8.5g⁵ 10.4f a10g Sep 1 He had a good break over the winter and has been gelded. He has done well physically and I'm really pleased with the horse. We are aiming to run him at the end of February in a listed race at Lingfield, and, hopefully, if he goes well, he could be a Winter Derby horse.

Planteur (Ire) (122) 6 b.h Danehill Dancer (Ire) – Plante Rare (Ire) (Giant's Causeway (USA)) 2012 a10g³ 9.3m² 10m 10.4m Aug 22 He had a setback at the end of last year, that's why he didn't run later in the season, but we are happy with him now, he's in good form and training well. The plan is to run on Super Saturday and then in the Dubai World Cup (third last year) on March 30 again.

Solar Deity (Ire) (100) 4 b.c Exceed And Excel (AUS) – Dawn Raid (Ire) (Docksider (USA)) 2012 p7m⁴ 6d⁴ 8g⁵ 7s 7.1m⁶ p7.1m* p8g* :: 2013 p7.1f³ p8m* Feb 16 I wasn't at all surprised he won off a BHA mark of 92 at Lingfield in February, as when he was third at Wolverhampton in January things didn't really work out for him, he raced wide and got going too late. He's a horse who had a few niggling problems last year, so we gave him a break and he's done well since. He's in the Lincoln (currently around 16/1).

Spifer (Ire) (95§) 5 gr.g Motivator – Zarawa (Ire) (Kahyasi) 2012 12g 12g⁶ 12m⁴ 14.1v p10g⁶ p9.5f³ :: 2013 p11g* Jan 19 He's a nice horse, if a little bit tricky. Obviously he's only won twice, but I think we've finally found the key to him. We learnt a lot from when he was third at Wolverhampton in December: he's a horse who just needs to challenge late. I thought that was a good run when he won a class 3 at Kempton in January, so hopefully he will regain some confidence and we can aim for some nice handicaps over a mile and a quarter or a mile and three furlongs.

Three-Year-Olds

Grendisar (Ire) (74p) 3 b.c Invincible Spirit (Ire) – Remarkable Story (Mark of Esteem (Ire)) 2012 8s 10.4v⁵ p8.6g p10f² :: 2013 p10m* Jan 10 He's a horse who wants a trip, a mile and a quarter plus. He still looked a little bit green when winning a class 5 handicap at Lingfield in January, so hopefully he will improve with time.

Holy Warrior (Ire) (88p) 3 b.c Holy Roman Emperor (Ire) – If Dubai (USA) (Stephen Got Even (USA)) 2012 NR :: 2013 p7m* Jan 24 He's not very big, but's he's a bonny horse and we like him a lot. I thought he would have a good chance in the maiden at Kempton on his debut (beat next-time-out winner Great Demeanor by three and a quarter lengths) and he's quite a useful horse.

Magical Kingdom (Ire) (82p) 3 b.c Danehill Dancer (Ire) – Al Saqiya (USA) (Woodman (USA)) 2012 NR :: 2013 p11m* Jan 23 He's owned by Coolmore and is a big horse, a stayer; there's plenty of stamina in his family and he's a half-brother to the likes of mile-and-a-half winner Homeric. It may have been a weak maiden but I though he won well at Kempton on his debut (beat El Massivo by two and three quarter lengths); considering his size I actually thought he would improve for the run. He travelled smoothly and picked up well that day, and I believe his opening mark of 77 is one that he can win off. I'm hopeful he will progress.

March (89) 3 b.f Dutch Art – Royal Pardon (Royal Applause) 2012 6g^4 p6m^3 5f* 5.1d* **Oct 10** She is a nice filly who, obviously, has plenty of speed. I think probably five or six furlongs will be her best trip.

Moohaajim (Ire) (116p) 3 b.c Cape Cross (Ire) – Thiella (USA) (Kingmambo (USA)) 2012 6m* 6g^5 6m* 6g^2 **Oct 13** He's in good form and has wintered really well. I think he has grown a little bit. If things go to plan we will probably run in the Greenham and then hopefully the Guineas. I don't think he'll have a problem with getting the mile—it should actually be his best trip on breeding.

Moohaajim (number 7) will be aimed at the 2,000 Guineas

Senafe (88) 3 b.f Byron – Kiruna (Northern Park (USA)) 2012 6g 6d^3 7m* 7v* **Jul 14** I think she will appreciate a step up to a mile this year. She's a tough filly, but she had a setback after she won a class 2 nursery at Newmarket in July so we had to just give her a break. She has done well through the winter and I'm really pleased with her. Whether she will develop into a stakes performer I'm not sure, but she is quite a scopey filly so we are hopeful. She's done well for a cheap purchase (cost 3,000 gns as a yearling).

FUTURE STARS

Michael Appleby

Some might say putting Michael Appleby in this list is akin to shutting the stable door after the horse has bolted, after the trainer, who actually saddled his initial Flat runners in 2004, sent out forty winners on the level in 2012, including Art Scholar in the November Handicap. However, a first treble (at odds of 702/1) at Lingfield just before Christmas—Hot Sugar (bought for £800 less than two months earlier) was backed from 33/1 to 12/1 and Royal Peculiar had only recently joined the trainer from Sir Henry Cecil—was further evidence, if it were needed, that Appleby's star is firmly in the ascendency.

Art Scholar was bought for just £600 having shown very little for Gary Moore after his winning debut, but he was quickly transformed into a progressive handicapper by Appleby, winning six of his next fifteen starts. More recently, Art Scholar, whose big Doncaster win came off a BHA mark some 41 lb higher than when starting out for his current trainer, became the Nottinghamshire operation's first runner at the Dubai Carnival. While following up such a fantastic campaign won't be easy, the confirmation that Andrew Mullen will ride as stable jockey suggests Appleby is laying down the foundations of an enterprise that will continue to flourish for many seasons to come.

Trainer's View: I would be delighted if we could match last year's total of winners, but my main aim this year will be to try and saddle more winners at the big meetings. The horse that I think could improve this year and win a big one is Demora (93), who ended last season on a high with wins in a couple of five-furlong handicaps.

Seamus Durack

As has been pointed out on many occasions, there seems to be a growing trend of jump jockeys carving out second careers as successful Flat trainers. Messrs O'Meara, Fahey, Ryan, Dascombe and Varian would be notable examples, but Seamus Durack, who partnered more than four hundred winners over the sticks and rode in a race as recently as May 2011 before another bad injury forced him to quit, is making an impression with far lesser resources and should be monitored closely over the next few campaigns.

Durack achieved just a single success from forty-one runners from saddling his first in 2010 to the end of 2011, but last year may well have represented a breakthrough. The trainer sent out seven winners from seventy-seven runners and caught the eye with his handling of Qaraaba, who he'd purchased as a Shadwell cast-off for just 11,000 gns early in her three-year-old year. Despite Qaraaba reaching the racecourse just four times over the next two years, Durack had the foresight (and patience!) required to see her bloom as a five-year-old last term, when she won three handicaps and finished a close fourth in a listed race at Royal Ascot. His belief in the mare –'I wanted to pick out a horse who could go on and be a proper 'Saturday horse' to put me on the map, and even when I bought her I had Royal Ascot in mind,'—was further vindicated when she went on to win a Grade 3 at Santa Anita, not needing to improve, on her second start for Simon Callaghan.

Trainer's View: We are looking forward to the coming year as we are due to move to a new yard in Upper Lambourn in March. We should have about twenty horses to call on in total through the year, which is nearly double what we had last year. We have been busy enough at the sales and have made a few nice purchases, I believe. I am looking forward to Linguine (92) who had a good level of form as a two-year-old last year for Charlie Hills. He is not very tall but has filled out considerably over the winter and looks a lot stronger. We also purchased the unexposed Altaria (84) and a very decent French recruit called Litigant (94p), both of whom I am looking forward to as dual-purpose horses. Kelpie Blitz (83) did well last year and should progress further this time. He has taken his time to grow up mentally but has always shown a bit of class at home and is only now beginning to strengthen up. I'm confident he will stay a mile and a half this year and would make a smashing hurdler if that discipline ever became an option.

Olly Stevens

Raised in Newmarket, Olly Stevens long harboured the desire to become a racehorse trainer and thanks to spells working for Jessica Harrington (twelve months), James Fanshawe (three years) and Keeneland-based Kellyn Gorder (five years) his dream is now a reality. Stevens, who saw Gorder's string expand from six to seventy horses during his employment, also met his wife Hetta while working for the trainer and it was her having worked for David Redvers at the sales that led to an incredible opportunity.

Redvers is the racing manager for Sheikh Fahad Al Thani's racing enterprises and recommended to the owner that Stevens, in his early-thirties, was the right man to take the reins at the fifty-box Robins Farm in Surrey, just an hour outside of London and purchased by the young member of the Qatari ruling family in the first half of 2012. Stevens will begin his first season with over thirty horses in training, of which over twenty are owned by Sheikh Fahad, and the same number being juveniles; 'The emphasis, initially, will be on sharpish two year-olds, which, historically, is what Robins Farm has excelled at,' says the handler. Stevens got off the mark with just his second runner when the much improved Hard Walnut landed the odds in a maiden at Lingfield in February, and it is only a matter of time before his name is being mentioned positively in betting shops up and down the country.

Trainer's View: Extortionist looks to have the makings of a sharp two-year-old and has impressed us all at home. He will be targeted at some of the earlier five-furlong races, while Hoku and a youngster by Camacho out of Inourhearts both look forward enough to go five furlongs, but will most likely be held up until the six furlong races start. Hoku is a very masculine filly and the Camacho looks athletic. Of our older horses Jacob Cats (106, a 240,000 gns purchase out of Richard Hannon's yard) stands out on form and will be campaigned towards heritage handicaps, while The Art of Racing (83) broke his maiden well at York and we hope he can shape up into a useful sprint handicapper. Uncle Muf is a big, rangy colt who was immature last year, but he is training well and could be a 'surprise package'.

David Bergin

David Bergin recorded an impressive sixteen wins in his first year riding on these shores last season but it would be no shock to see him better that in 2013. Bergin, who had partnered one winner from thirty-seven rides in his native Ireland when based with David Marnane, first appeared in a British racecard in late-June and soon looked good value for his 7 lb claim. Bergin rode four winners and four seconds from his first eleven mounts before landing hat-tricks aboard both Fear Nothing and Aubrietia for his new boss David O'Meara and he also partnered the trainer's Elusive Bonus to win four handicaps before the season was over.

The upwardly mobile O'Meara has supplied Bergin with the lion's share of his mounts in Britain so far, but he has also ridden winners for Alan McCabe among others, and taken mounts on horses trained by such as Richard Fahey and James Given—clearly he has the potential to become one of the best apprentice jockeys in the North in the near future. The fact that Bergin was only seen sparingly on the all-weather over the winter—he more or less rode exclusively for O'Meara—suggests that those in his corner want to preserve his allowance for the turf season ahead, and his services could be well sought after in some of the season's more notable handicaps.

George Downing

The apprentice handicap that closes the Champions' Day card at Ascot may not be everyone's cup of tea, but it's a race that will have fond memories for George Downing as his win on the ultra-progressive Jack Dexter last October was accompanied with a rather special prize. Downing, based with Worcestershire handler Tony Carroll, was handed a month's work experience with ex-pat trainer Simon Callaghan and spent December at Santa Anita Park, California.

If his trip Stateside has improved Downing in any way he will be a force to be reckoned with this campaign as he rode seventeen winners (for seven different trainers) last year, doing so at a seventeen per cent strike rate and making his supporters a profit to level stakes. Those statistics are made even more impressive by the fact that he spent almost three months on the sidelines having sustained a broken jaw and a fractured skull when falling at Kempton in June. Downing highlighted his skills when winning a handicap on Edgeworth, a horse who hadn't won for over a year, last summer and the combination of sound judgement of pace and strength in the saddle he showed that day will surely see him in the winners enclosure plenty more times throughout the course of this season.

Ryan Tate

Ryan Tate is the son of former jockey Jason and is attached to the Clive Cox yard in Lambourn. Winner of one race in 2011 and three during the turf season in 2012, Tate's talents were really showcased on the all-weather over the winter, with his success aboard the fast-finishing Travelling in an apprentice race at Kempton highlighting that in terms of both tactical awareness and style he's ahead of a lot of his peers. Tate also secured his first double that day when winning the next race aboard the Hans Adielsson-trained Compton Rainbow; it was Tate's first time on the improved filly, who was landing a maiden on her twelfth start, and the second time in just over a week that the jockey had ridden two consecutive winners.

Aside from Cox—who has strongly supported young jockeys such as Adam Kirby, Luke Morris and John Fahy in recent years and who describes his protégé as 'very good value for his 7 lb'—Tate has ridden for at least two dozen trainers already, including such as Marco Botti, Gary Moore, Hughie Morrison and Tony Carroll. The last-named ended a seventy-one-race losing streak when Tate scored aboard Travelling at the beginning of the year, while less than a week earlier the rider had been chosen by trainer Robert Mills to partner the gambled-on Club House—a horse ridden to victory over the winter by another promising apprentice in Robert Tart—at Lingfield, the duo winning by a head. Tate is a young jockey going places and it would a surprise if he doesn't enhance his reputation appreciably in 2013.

CLASSIC ANTE-POST

Timeform's Chief Correspondent Jamie Lynch casts his eye over the ante-post markets for the 2013 classics, as well as taking a typically novel approach to finding where the value lies in the Champion Jockey market...

In 4,500,000,000 AD, or thereabouts, the world will end. The art of long-range forecasting is, by its nature, haphazard at best and fraudulent at worst, though the above prophesy does at least have some basis in science, as the sun will eventually incinerate the earth according to calculations by the men in white coats; not the same men in white coats who should have been dispatched to Bugarach, France last December to herd up the loonies and nutters who believed in the Mayan Apocalypse.

You could see—courtesy of the camera crews that were, equally ridiculously, sent at great expense to cover this nonsense—in these weirdos' eyes that they believed, really believed, in the December 21 doomsday, including the part about the pilgrims being rescued by aliens hidden inside the mountain. Have you ever wondered what these people do once the 'place remains unaltered' announcement has been made and they realise they've backed a loser? Rather than being forced to embark on a countrywide Olympic torch-style relay, whereby they run through the streets wearing nothing but a dunce's cap while normal people hurl abuse and various vegetables at them, which is clearly what should happen, I suspect the deceived disciples are allowed to just shrug their shoulders and slope off with impunity.

With the words 'let he who is without sin cast the first stone' ringing in my ears, it's my prophetic task, taking the General Melchett role, to tactically line up some of our highlighted horses in a classics battleplan. Baaah! If the dunce's cap fits, I might be the one running the gauntlet, but whether or not we pinpoint any classic winners, remember that it's not the end of the world...not until 4,500,000,000.

2000 Guineas

The odds are probably less than 4,500,000,000/1 that in the year 4,500,000,000 the favourite for the first colts' classic will be named [insert] Approach and trained by [insert] Bolger, given their strike rate in recent years; first was 'New' in 2008 and now there's his son 'Dawn', both champion two-year-olds for 'Jim'. New failed in the Guineas before winning the Derby, but it's more likely to be the other way round for Dawn, according to Jim, and the betting. The numbers six, one and eight suggest **Dawn Approach** will win the Guineas: six races unbeaten, ranked one in the world for his age by Timeform, and bound to be suited by eight furlongs. So why take him on?

As General Melchett said: 'If nothing else works, a total pig-headed unwillingness to look facts in the face will see us through.' There is that, but also Dawn Approach hasn't looked quite so bombproof as his perfect record would suggest, and for each win he's traded at bigger odds in-running, highlighting a lazyish side; a lazyish side that might just be exposed more in a Guineas on what's likely to be his first race of the season.

Moohaajim (blue cap) looks the standout bet for the 2000 Guineas at this stage

Furthermore, the opposition will be better than he generally met last year, principally **Kingsbarns**, whose uncanny impression of Camelot should earn him more awards in 2013, though his major role is probably in the Derby, while stablemate **Mars** remains a massive guess-up. The home defence is considered to rest on Richard Hannon's shoulders, with **Olympic Glory** and **Toronado**, but there is another British-trained youngster with equivalent form and arguably greater potential. The twice (from four starts) **Moohaajim** was beaten last year was in Group 1 races, both times behind the very speedy Reckless Abandon over six furlongs, but going down by only a neck latterly, in the the Middle Park at Newmarket.

His form as it stands entitles him to be shorter than the 25/1 available, but Moohaajim's build and pedigree strongly suggest he'll make a better three-year-old over longer trips. Marco Botti has told us that he'll follow the Exceleration path by starting out in the Greenham at Newbury, and if Moohaajim wins that—and he will—then he'll halve in price for the main event. With his sprinting background, Moohaajim will be armed and ready to jump all over any flat spots, meaning a flat spot of bother for Dawn Approach.

Recommendation: Moohaajim

1000 Guineas

Certify is the one on trial here, and the evidence is stacked against her. The problem isn't so much her as Godolphin, for whom White Moonstone, Lyric of Light and Discourse are Exhibits A, B and C as fillies who didn't train on at all. But, using another Melchett line, 'before we sentence the deceased, I mean defendant, I think we had better hear from the prosecution.' Certify was the best in her division last year, as testified by four starts unbeaten, including the Group 1 Fillies' Mile. All the same, besides guilt by association, in terms of Godolphin's former flopping fillies, Certify hasn't the physique nor the pedigree to guarantee her proving as good a three-year-old. She'll start at 16/1, if she gets there at all.

One who won't start at 16/1—though that's the mouthwatering price she is now with some firms—is **Big Break**. Dermot Weld has won most big races around the world, the 1000 Guineas one of the few unticked boxes (he's won the Irish version four times), but Big Break looks qualified to put that right, based on her smooth success from a field that included colts in the Killavullan Stakes at Leopardstown. There's a famous name in her family, namely Famous Name (likewise trained by Weld), whose class, hunger and strike rate—he won twenty-one of thirty-eight starts—are positive recommendations for his not-so-little sister.

With the exception of **What A Name**, who like Big Break took on the colts, only better ones in her case when runner-up to Olympic Glory in a Group 1 in her native France, none of the other established performers have the X Factor, and therefore it could pay to look at the next wave of girl power, to swap that Emeli Sande ticket for an A*M*E* one (trust me, I caught a bit of Radio 1 the other day). For A*M*E* see **Winsili**, whose appearances up to now have been low-key but high-interest. She had to miss the Fillies' Mile, withdrawn on the day, but her entry said plenty, especially given the stable, that of champion trainer John Gosden. A small investment now in Winsili (she's available at 33/1) may prove shrewd come the Nell Gwyn Stakes, Gosden's preferred trial, a race he's won three times.

There's the grey area of how quickly the respective fillies will come to hand, but it's black and white as far as our hopes and expectations are concerned as to who'll blossom when—Certify-slow, Big Break-fast, possibly with egg (on our face).

Recommendation: Big Break

The Derby

The only issue with **Kingsbarns** is that he's already 5/1 and therefore not very sexy. Secure, yes. Sexy, no. But there's nothing wrong with a bit of security. We're back with Melchett again: 'Security isn't a dirty word, Blackadder. Crevice is a dirty word, but security isn't.' All the same, that's not what we're here for, to tell you that the favourite has a good chance in the Derby. The purpose of long-range betting is to identify a small dot that might become a big dot on the radar by June 1. We need something to magnify a small dot. A **Telescope**, perhaps?

One of Timeform's shortlisted ten within the *Fifty*, signifying our belief in him, Telescope's lyricals have been well and truly waxed in his main entry, suffice to say we're anticipating him staking, and indeed enhancing, his Derby claims in the Dante at York in May. If that steak is well done, the 14s will be rare. If you only back one out of this whole preview, make sure it's the horse with all the scope, the Telescope.

A second then a first in autumn maidens, barely scratching the surface of his ability, hence the Timeform large 'P', and from a smart family and a Derby-winning yard, **Zand** is identical to Telescope in profile, but more than twice the price in the ante-post market, a price worth taking. Picked out by our Irish team, albeit the same Irish team who overlooked Sea The Stars in the 2009 publication, Zand is bred on the same cross (by Zamindar out of a Kahyasi mare) as the unstoppable Zarkava, and the quote from John Oxx in Zand's write-up, specifically the mentioning of the

Ballysax, which Oxx has generally used as a stepping stone to Epsom, seems a statement of Derby intent.

Recommendations: Telescope, Zand

The Oaks

If this were a podcast—and, who knows, it may be one day given the advent of the microphone—then this is the point at which the accent would go from a gentle Geordie lilt to the rough, gruff of East Yorkshire, as **Secret Gesture** is Martin Dixon's baby. Our Chief Reporter was so taken with Secret Gesture's two juvenile runs that he even shut up about Hull City FC for five minutes to snap up the 50s and 33s for the Oaks. There's still some 33/1 available, but the football season ends in May. Well bred, physically attractive and a keen sort, if a little headstrong, Martin can be spotted on various racecourses throughout the year, so you know who to thank or throttle.

Of the ante-post favourites, we've discussed the pros of **Big Break** and the cons of **Certify**, though Big Break wouldn't be sure to stay a mile and a half, whereas it will be the making of **Liber Nauticus**. The stewards enquiry is ongoing as to how she didn't make the cut for the *Fifty* itself, but there's only one race for her anyway, and this is it. With each yard of the Goodwood maiden she won on her only start, Liber Nauticus looked more and more an Oaks filly, and she's certainly bred for the job, being by Azamour and from the family of Conduit.

Recommendations: Secret Gesture, Liber Nauticus

'Ah, tally-ho, yippety-dip and zing zang spillip. Are you looking forward to the big push?' After this classic preview, General Melchett, I think we are. Baaah!

JOCKEYS' CHAMPIONSHIP

Dr David Seftel, an American specialist in jockeys' health, has called it an 'extraordinary situation' whereby 'you effectively have mandated malnutrition,' while Hall of Fame jockey Kent Desormeaux claimed that '85% of riders are dying to ride – literally.' Jockeys and hunger are intertwined in a dangerous issue; dangerous as much because it's easily neglected, taken for granted as part of the game, an outdated part of the game perhaps, but in Britain there has at least been a nod in that direction with the minimum Flat riding weight increased by 2 lb to eight stone this year. Hunger in that sense is a hardship forced upon most riders, but the other type of hunger, the overwhelming desire to win, is what makes a champion jockey. Ability, opportunity, backing and soundness are, of course, all key components, but hunger - the willingness to ride a dozen horses at two tracks on most days - is more often than not the determining factor.

Of those still riding, Hughes, Hanagan, Moore, Fallon, Spencer, Dettori and Sanders have all, at some time, shown the compulsory commitment, though recently Spencer has taken his foot off the pedal, Fallon and Dettori have had their foot taken off the pedal, and Sanders has taken to peddling nearer the foot of the league. Among the accelerators, with their tail up and foot down, are Buick, de Sousa and, newest of all, Lee. So how do we go about assessing the contenders, from the former winners to the formative winners? Option 1 was an elaborate statistical breakdown using complex algorithms to calculate ride-number and strike-rate projection based on historical data of the individual jockey and their top-three connected trainers, factoring in recency variance and odds expectation. Option 2 was a child's game.

Simple and recreational, using cards with comparable values to help conclude who may come up trumps as top rider in the numbers game that is the jockeys' championship, Timeform is proud to present *Hot Jocks*, which for legal reasons is nothing like a long-established, similar-sounding, card-based game of relative data. Let's look at the six high cards in *Hot Jocks*, incorporating prices, records, strengths, weaknesses, allies and special moves, to settle where the value lies.

RICHARD HUGHES

Odds	Evens
2012	177 wins
Strength	Artistry, a joy to watch
Weakness	Daunted by the fight?
Ally	Hannon and his 200-odd winners
Special Move	'The Sidler'
	Sidling through a field on the bridle

RYAN MOORE

Odds	7/2
2012	116 wins (missed six weeks through injury)
Strength	Being Ryan Moore
Weakness	Injuries, O'Brien link
Ally	Widespread demand
Special Move	'The Finisher'
	Rarely loses a tight finish

GRAHAM LEE

Odds	12/1
2012	108 wins
Strength	Tactician the right-place-right-time knack
Weakness	The South
Ally	The North
Special Move	'The Go-To'
	The go-to man when the south comes north

WILLIAM BUICK

Odds	7/1
2012	130 wins
Strength	Hunger
Weakness	Ammunition
Ally	The champion trainer
Special Move	'The Extricater'
	Ability to get out of tight spots

PAUL HANAGAN

Odds	20/1
2012	122 wins
Strength	Attitude
Weakness	Married to the job, the Hamdan job
Ally	Experience
Special Move	'The T-Shirt'
	Been there and done that. Twice.

SILVESTRE DE SOUSA

Odds	7/1
2012	145 wins
Strength	Strength
Weakness	Attachments
Ally	Mickael Barzalona
Special Move	'The Persister'
	Persistence often pays off

It's easy to see why Richard Hughes is favourite to regain the title, and short at that, with the same conveyor-belt stable behind him and without the handicap start like in 2012 when a ban picked up in India left him on the blocks until May. However, Hughes' odds of even-money don't reflect that some things are different, or at least likely to be different, from last year, possibly including his win-at-all-costs mindset. Hughes, by his own admission, went through the mill to get his name on the roll of honour, having tried (very hard) and failed (very narrowly) against Hanagan in 2011, and his statement on this year's championship bid that he'll 'chip away until Goodwood and then go hell for leather if there with a shout' is hardly a statement brimming with intent that will have you rushing to the bookies. And there's more: Ryan Moore.

Moore could do with a break, and not the sort of break that has put paid to his challenge in each of the three seasons since he won back-to-back titles (2008/9). Let's not overlook the fact that when injury struck him last year, in late-August, Moore was still four clear of Hughes. Some will point to Sir Michael Stoute as a well that might be drying up, but he provided less than a third of Moore's 2012 total, anyway, with twenty-nine other trainers supplying winners and a further fifty-two giving him rides, highlighting the value of Moore's currency, which is an obvious plus when the chase is on. After three years of shortened rations, Moore will be hungry, maybe hungrier than Hughes.

Hanagan and de Sousa are likely too tied by their retainers, while Buick's prospects depend on John Gosden having an even better 2013 than 2012, which is bigger than 7/1, and that brings us to Graham Lee, who probably should be shorter than 12s. On the Flat, this is his sophomore season, which is always harder, or so the cliché goes, but Lee has momentum on his side, as well as geography. Lee could mop up in the North, the way he increasingly did through last year, and the way Hanagan did on his way to the title in '10 and '11. Richard Fahey was the kingmaker those times, and though there's been no sign nor hint of an association so far, it wouldn't be a surprise if the Northern stars of Lee and Fahey gravitated towards each other this year.

Though game cards in name, *Hot Jocks* are more Tarot cards in practice, needing to be interpreted, and my reading of them is that Hughes is too short and Lee is too big but **Ryan Moore** is the one to bet on. Given luck – not good luck, just less bad luck than in recent years - 'The Finisher' will be out in force in 2013.

BACK ON THE LEVEL

Horses who had previously run under National Hunt rules have won the Chester Cup for the last three years, claimed three of the last five Northumberland Plates and landed six renewals of the Cesarewitch since the turn of the century, which means punters need to make themselves fully aware of some of the likely types for this season's big staying handicap honours. With that in mind, here are some horses we believe can win races back on the level in the coming months having spent the winter over jumps...

Big handicap wins for Overturn, Ile de Re and Lexi's Boy over the last couple of years mean Donald McCain is the first port of call when it comes to narrowing down this list, and one of the most obvious contenders to follow in their footsteps is **Hollow Tree**. A Grade 1 win as a juvenile means Hollow Tree is poorly handicapped over timber but the mud-loving five-year-old, who landed a second successive three-year-old handicap over a mile and three quarters at Sandown for Andrew Balding when last seen on the Flat, can revert to racing on the level off an attractive-looking BHA mark of 80. **Counsel** was steadily progressive for Sir Michael Stoute in the first half of 2012, winning a ten-furlong handicap on polytrack before selling to McCain for 40,000 gns, and he too could be well treated if reverting back having landed a couple of races over hurdles during the winter. Others from Bankhouse to look out for are three-time winner at a mile and three quarters Veloce, consistent middle-distance handicapper Life And Soul, Simenon's half-brother Right To Rule, and fairly useful pair Aazif and Trend Is My Friend.

John Quinn-trained juvenile hurdlers **Calculated Risk**, **Hidden Justice** and **Kashmir Peak** all got their second careers off to the perfect start, the first-named beating Aazif comfortably at Doncaster, the second-named readily winning at Wetherby (Mashaari only fourth) and the last-named winning at Market Rasen before improving plenty to take a Grade 2 at Doncaster (Counsel fourth). Like the trainer's 2012 Triumph Hurdle winner/Cesarewitch runner-up Countrywide Flame, all look shrewd purchases who could easily make a deeper impact reverted to the Flat. Calculated Risk, who won a ten-furlong handicap off an official rating of 59 last July for Willie Musson, is now on 67 and Hidden Justice, who stays a mile and three quarters and was second off 69 on his final start for Amanda Perrett in October, is currently rated 73. Kashmir Peak also won a handicap over a mile and a quarter in 2012, for Ger Lyons at Navan in May.

In 2011/12 Brian Ellison had the most winners he'd ever had in a season as a trainer over jumps, while the 2012 Flat campaign also brought a career-best in terms of number of successes. In other words, his horses are very much worth following across both disciplines. Dual hurdles winner **Totalize** catches the eye as he was beaten only by subsequent Grade 1 scorer **Ruacana** (another potential code switcher to watch out for) on his debut over timber and has actually been dropped 2 lb to a BHA mark of 84 on the Flat since finishing mid-field in a handicap at Lingfield, his fourth race in quick succession and his last before selling for 50,000 gns out of the Luca Cumani yard. **Mashaari** has so far failed to meet expectations over obstacles but the two-and-a-quarter-mile York handicap winner was being talked of as a potential Plate horse by Ellison after he bought him for 160,000 gns in October, and it would be no surprise to see him landing another race or two granted testing conditions.

Finally, a couple a bit more out of left field are Sheena West's Feb Thirtyfirst and Hughie Morrison's Cousin Khee. **Feb Thirtyfirst** showed very little in five starts at up to twelve furlongs on the Flat and it may just be that he's a better hurdler—he won two of his first four starts and was then fourth to Ruacana at the highest level—but the fact that he's officially rated some 74 lb lower on the level means he's worth keeping a close eye on all the same. Six-year-old **Cousin Khee** only made his Flat debut in February having been a fairly useful bumper performer, but he got off the mark in impressive fashion next time and is open to further improvement on the level.

VIEW FROM THE COURSE

Timeform's Chief Reporter Martin Dixon has already made no secret of his admiration for Secret Gesture, one of our 'Fifty', earlier in this book, and he picks out another three horses who caught his eye more than most during his travels in 2012...

Emerald Sea (69p) 3 b.f Green Desert (USA) – Wind Surf (USA) (Lil's Lad (USA)) 2012 6s 6g⁵ Aug 9 Emerald Sea may have been beaten a combined seventeen lengths in two starts as a two-year-old but she is a lengthy and attractive filly with plenty of scope and expected to advance her form appreciably in 2013. The second foal of a winning miler in the States, from the family of British/French 1000 Guineas winner Ravinella, Emerald Sea was considerately handled in strong maidens at Newmarket (won by Certify) and Yarmouth (won by useful Taayel), but the fact that she started at just 9/4 for the latter despite having been sent off at 50/1 at HQ is eye-catching. As pointed out elsewhere in these pages, Chris Wall has an impressive record with his three-year-olds in handicaps over the last five seasons and Emerald Sea, who needs one more run to qualify for a BHA mark, can make a healthy contribution to his total this time round. *Chris Wall*

Mukhadram (109p) 4 b.c Shamardal (USA) – Magic Tree (UAE) (Timber Country (USA)) 2012 8d* 8g* 10d⁴ 8s² 9g⁵ Sep 29 The strong Mukhadram impressed in appearance on numerous occasions in 2012, and strikes as one who is yet to reach his full potential. A half-brother to mile-and-a-half winner Entihaa (by Tiger Hill), who himself only made his debut in April last year aged four, Mukhadram quickly made up into a useful performer last term, winning at Newmarket on his first two starts, though his success in the Wood Ditton first time out was retrospective owing to the disqualification of first-past-the-post Mariner's Cross. A fourth at Royal Ascot (to Energizer in the Tercentenary Stakes) and a second to the smart

Sovereign Debt, beaten two lengths, in a minor event on the July Course meant Mukhadram was sent off just 10/1 for the Cambridgeshire on his handicap debut. Mukhadram may have been beaten only two and three quarter lengths in finishing fifth of thirty-three to Bronze Angel, but he looked a likely winner until his effort flattened out two furlongs out and was possibly just in need of the run after eleven weeks off. The strong-travelling Mukhadram, who often races prominently, is undoubtedly a pattern performer in the making and can make a name for himself at between a mile and ten furlongs this season. He's raced only on good ground or softer so far (acts on soft). *William Haggas*

Tajheez (Ire) (65p) 3 b.g Raven's Pass (USA) – Ghaidaa (Ire) (Cape Cross (Ire)) 2012 8s 8.3v 8.3v³ Nov 7 Being a first foal doesn't seem to have held Tajheez back in terms of physique as he's a strong sort who really took the eye on the course last year, looking every inch one who would make up into a much better three-year-old. That's just as well for his connections as Tajheez showed little better than modest form in three maidens, easily his best effort coming when a well-held third of thirteen to Dashing Star at Nottingham, but his finishing positions did not tell the whole story. Tajheez was seemingly being brought along slowly, residual greenness still visible last time, and he could prove to be very well handicapped starting the new season from an official mark of just 62, with a gelding operation since his final outing likely to have aided his progression. Out of a ten-furlong winner who is closely related to such as smart nine- to twelve-furlong winner Itnab and a half-sister to Oaks heroine Eswarah, Tajheez is likely to stay a mile and a quarter. *Roger Varian*

View From The Course is a regular feature in Horses To Follow Extra, which is published ten times a season to coincide with the big meetings.

FIRST-SEASON SIRES

Aqlaam (Highest Timeform Rating 125)
Oasis Dream – Bourbonella (Rainbow Quest (USA))

William Haggas described Aqlaam as 'a colt blessed with natural speed, true ability and an exceptional temperament—an incredibly genuine horse', and judged on his sales results in 2012, he could well make an impression as a sire this term. Twenty-four of Aqlaam's yearlings changed hands for an average of over 45,000 gns, with the second highest-priced (a colt out of listed winner Firebelly named Taanif) being purchased for 125,000 gns by Aqlaam's owner Hamdan Al Maktoum, who is sure to give the stallion plenty of help in his second career.

Seen out just once as a two-year-old and only twice in a three-year-old season that saw him unbeaten in two races, including the Jersey Stakes, Aqlaam landed the Prix du Moulin at four years, beating Famous Name (takes up stallion duties in 2013) and Virtual (first two-year-olds this term). Aqlaam also finished a creditable third to Paco Boy in the Queen Anne and runner-up to Goldikova in the Prix Jacques le Marois. The lengthy, quite attractive Aqlaam, whose fee has remained at £7,000 since he began covering in 2010, is also represented in his first crop by a half-brother to Wootton Bassett and a half-sister to listed winner Senor Mirasol.

Bushranger (119)
Danetime (Ire) – Danz Danz (Efisio)

The smallish, good-bodied Bushranger may not have trained on at three years but he was a smart two-year-old who won the Prix Morny and the Middle Park, and he looks set to be well represented on the track in his first season as a sire. Bushranger, whose stud fee for 2013 is back up to the €7,500 at which he covered his first mares, had one hundred of his progeny sell at European auctions last year, some twenty-three more than any other stallion. Despite such market saturation, they averaged at a rather impressive 37,580 gns.

Noting those who purchased Bushranger's yearlings, we can expect to see his juveniles running for the likes of Richard Hannon, Jeremy Noseda, Kevin Ryan and Charlie Hills this term, and that, allied to his large crop, means Bushranger is in a strong position to be leading first-season sire in terms of number of winners, and possibly prize money. Certainly, the breeders who made him the busiest Flat stallion in 2012 by sending him two hundred and fifteen mares will be hoping so!

Intense Focus (117)
Giant's Causeway (USA) – Daneleta (Ire) (Danehill (USA))

Winners of the Dewhurst over the last twenty years have a mixed record at stud, with a handful headed by the likes of Zafonic and Grand Lodge just outweighing the Distant Musics, Tobouggs and Milk It Micks. The recent examples of Dewhurst winners Teofilo and New Approach, and, to a lesser extent Group 3 scorer Heliostatic, point to Intense Focus being well supported by his trainer Jim Bolger, while another positive is that he had forty-six first-crop yearlings sell for an average of over 20,000 gns.

The 2008 Dewhurst, in which he was visored for the first time having been blinkered on his previous three starts, was Intense Focus's ninth race of the season and he won a substandard renewal by a nose and the same from Lord Shanakill and Finjaan. Intense Focus failed to match that form in two outings as a three-year-old, showing a questionable attitude when fifth in the St James's Palace on the latter occasion, and was retired to Ballylinch Stud for 2010. Described as 'a beautifully conformed and very correct horse…as befits a very fast two-year-old he should have a strong influence for speed and precocity' by Ballylinch managing director John O'Connor, the neat Intense Focus should supply his fair share of juvenile winners.

Mastercraftsman (129)
Danehill Dancer (Ire) – Starlight Dreams (USA) (Black Tie Affair)

Mastercraftsman will be one of the highest-rated horses among this year's first-season sires, owing in part to his victory in the 2009 Irish 2000 Guineas. Mastercraftsman, who had won his first four starts as a juvenile, including the Phoenix Stakes (beat Art Connoisseur and Bushranger) and National Stakes, also landed the St James's Palace as a three-year-old, as well as finishing in the frame in the Juddmonte International, Irish Champion Stakes and the Breeders' Cup Dirt Mile. A genuine and consistent prominent racer who was precocious yet proved effective at up to an extended ten furlongs, it is unsurprising that Mastercraftsman was very popular in his first season at stud.

Mastercraftsman had seventy-five offspring sell at auction in Europe in 2012, realising an average of 46,806 gns (he stood at €20,000 when the mares were covered), and he provided the top lot at Doncaster's Premier Sales when a colt out of a half-sister to Arkansas Derby winner Archarcharch was purchased for £185,000 on behalf of the Coolmore partners. Mastercraftsman, a big, good sort who has shuttled to New Zealand for the last few seasons, will stand his fourth year at

Coolmore Stud in Ireland in 2013 and, while his fee has slipped to €12,500, it would be no shock to see him hit the headlines as a stallion in the near future.

Myboycharlie (118)
Danetime (Ire) – Dulceata (Ire) (Rousillon (USA))

Myboycharlie is already a winning producer as Charlie Boy got him off the mark when winning at Rosehill, Australia in November. It is not a surprise that Myboycharlie has made a bright start either as, similar to Bushranger (also by very smart sprinter Danetime) and Intense Focus, his best form was achieved as a juvenile.

The lengthy, quite good-topped and useful-looking Moyboycharlie won the Anglesey Stakes and the Prix Morny by a combined nine lengths, having transferred ownership to Messrs Magnier, Tabor and Smith prior to the latter. Myboycharlie couldn't confirm the form he showed in those races in the National Stakes (third to New Approach) and won only an optional claimer over a mile in the States at three years, but he has been well supported at stud and looks to have a future as a sire. From an initial fee of £5,500, Myboycharlie had forty-one progeny sell for an average of 34,148 gns in Europe last year, with such as Coolmore, John Warren and French trainer Jean-Claude Rouget among the buyers. His first crop contains the likes of a half-sister to triple Group 1 winner Sahpresa.

Sea The Stars (140)
Cape Cross (Ire) – Urban Sea (USA) (Miswaki (USA))

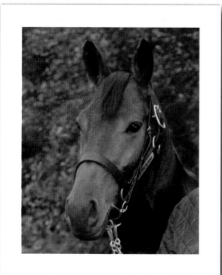

By far the most eagerly anticipated two-year-olds this year will be those sired by Sea The Stars, one of the highest-rated racehorses in Timeform's sixty-five year history, and it was no surprise that his yearlings (thirty-two) sold for an average of nearly a quarter of a million guineas last year, with two of the most expensive being Royal Battalion (out of a sister to Fame And Glory) and Altaayil.

The big and lengthy Sea The Stars, whose fee has remained at a constant €85,000, covered a cosmopolitan book of mares in his first season. They included high-class Japanese performer

Vodka and France's top-class, unbeaten Arc winner Zarkava, and the odds on any of his progeny winning a Group 1 in Europe this season are currently just 11/10 with one leading bookmaker. Sea The Stars' pedigree is crammed with fellow sires, as he is a half-brother to Galileo, Black Sam Bellamy and Born To Sea (covers his first mares in 2013), and from the family of King's Best, Anabaa Blue and Tamayuz.

Best of the rest

Plenty of speedy types are represented for the first time this season, including Royal Ascot-winning juveniles **Art Connoisseur** (Coventry) and **Winker Watson** (Norfolk), the latter having actually returned to the track in 2011 despite reportedly having no issues with fertility. It will be a surprise if they, along with the similarly precocious **Captain Gerrard**, **Dandy Man** and **Major Cadeaux**, can't fire in a winner or two, but whether any of them have the firepower to compete in the end-of-year standings either on number of winner of total prize money remains to be seen. Those likely to impart a bit more stamina to their offspring include high-class performer at up to a ten furlongs **Archipenko** and **Champs Elysees**, a brother to Cacique and Dansili who was effective at up to a mile and three quarters. Quadruple Gold Cup hero **Yeats** will also have his first runners in 2013.

SECTION

TIMEFORM'S VIEW

As a special guide to this year's classics, here is Timeform's detailed analysis— compiled by our team of race reporters and supplemented by observations from Timeform's handicappers—of a selection of key juvenile races from last year.

CURRAGH Sunday, Sep 9
GOOD

5732 Moyglare Stud Stks (Gr 1) (2yo f) £103,571   7f

5236²	SKY LANTERN (IRE) *RichardHannon,GB* 2-9-0		1
	RichardHughes (11)........................	7/1	
5272	SCINTILLULA (IRE) *JSBolger* 2-9-0 (t) *RPWhelan* (10)........	33/1	2½ 2
4797²	HARASIYA (IRE) *JohnMOxx* 2-9-0 *PatSmullen* (4)	3/1	hd 3
4797⁶	Magical Dream (IRE) *AidanO'Brien* 2-9-0 *SeamieHeffernan* (9) ...	16/1	½ 4
4795*	Starbright (IRE) *KevinPrendergast* 2-9-0 *CDHayes* (12)	14/1	1¾ 5
3766*	Sendmylovetorose *AndrewOliver* 2-9-0 *CO'Donoghue* (7)	9/2	nk 6
5297*	Karamaya (IRE) *JohnMOxx* 2-9-0 *NGMcCullagh* (5).........	16/1	1 7
4797³	Diamond Sky (IRE) *JSBolger* 2-9-0 *KJManning* (8)...........	20/1	½ 8
4814*	Orpha *MickChannon,GB* 2-9-0 *WilliamBuick* (1)	5/1	2¾ 9
2978*	Private Alexander (IRE) *GMLyons* 2-9-0 *GFCarroll* (6)	20/1	nk 10
4797⁵	Nandiga (USA) *PJPrendergast* 2-9-0 *DeclanMcDonogh* (2)......	50/1	8½ 11
5272*	Snow Queen (IRE) *AidanO'Brien* 2-9-0 (s) *JosephO'Brien* (13)...	11/1	1½ 12
4797*	My Special J'S (USA) *JohnPatrickShanahan* 2-9-0		nk 13
	JohnnyMurtagh (3).......................	9/2	

4.25race Mr B. Keswick 13ran 1m25.14

An open-looking renewal of this Group 1 for 2-y-o fillies and the biggest field since Quarter Moon saw off 16 rivals in 2001, one of the 3 supplementary entries becoming only the second British-trained winner this century and first since Mail The Desert 10 years ago; in bare form terms Sky Lantern produced a lesser effort than the last 2 winners, but she was impressive in settling the issue with a sharp turn of foot after the pace had taken a while to build. **Sky Lantern**, back away from softish ground, built on her earlier promise this time and resumed winning ways in good style; patiently ridden, travelled fluently, headway over 2f out, quickened to lead 1f out, drifted right, pushed out, will stay 1m; she is among the best of what presently looks an average bunch and there is little mileage in being too downbeat about her Guineas prospects at this stage given the big prices still available; she's reportedly being considered for the Breeders' Cup Juvenile Fillies Turf next. **Scintillula**, in a first-time tongue strap, showed useful form and had clearly learnt plenty from debut, comprehensively reversing form with Snow Queen; mid-field, pushed along over 2f out, took time to get going, finished well to take second on the line; will go on improving, banker for maiden, will be suited by 1m. **Harasiya** hasn't progressed as expected since winning her first 2 starts at Leopardstown; chased leaders, every chance over 1f out, not quicken. **Magical Dream**, on her first run away from testing ground, bounced back from a disappointing effort in the Debutante at C&D, confirming earlier Galway form with Diamond Sky; ridden more patiently, not ideally placed, pushed along over 2f out, stayed on, never nearer; will stay 1m. **Starbright**, back down in trip, ran about as well as could have been expected upped in grade; held up, forced to switch over 2f out, kept on, never landed a blow. **Sendmylovetorose** was beaten by more than this 1f longer trip after 9 weeks off, not good enough up in grade, and has seemingly reached limit in form terms; tracked pace, headway halfway, effort 2f out, no extra. **Karamaya** knew more than on her debut and had the run of the race, so it was disappointing she didn't improve more; made running, headed 1f out, no extra. **Diamond Sky** is better judged on previous form; dropped out, kept on, never on terms, had a hopeless task from its position; worth another chance, will stay 1m. **Orpha**, over this 1f longer trip, faced a stiffer task up sharply in grade and was seemingly nowhere near good enough; mid-field, driven over 2f out, made no impression. **Private Alexander** whose form last time isn't working out, needed to find plenty of improvement after 13 weeks off and was well held; close up, took keen hold, driven under 2f out, faded. **Nandiga** ran poorly, not up to the task; raced off the pace, driven halfway, merely passed beaten horses. **Snow Queen** lost all chance at the start, missed break by several lengths and went left, in touch after 2f, found little when shaken up 2f out, eased off; best treated with caution. **My Special J's** had 4 of these behind in the Debutante and this clearly wasn't her running; chased leaders, struggling 2f out, folded, not persevered with once held.

DONCASTER Saturday, Sep 15
GOOD

5894 One Call Insurance Champagne Stks 7f
(Gr 2) (1) (2yo c+g) £46,559

3996 ¹	TORONADO (IRE) *RichardHannon* 2-8-12 RichardHughes (1)	5/2 11/4		1
5154 ¹	DUNDONNELL (USA) *RogerCharlton* 2-8-12 JamesDoyle (5)	10/11 5/6f	½	2
5496 ²	THA'IR (IRE) *SaeedbinSuroor* 2-8-12 FrankieDettori (3)	5 9/2	2¼	3
4369	Maxentius (IRE) *PeterChapple-Hyam* 2-8-12 WilliamBuick (2)	14/1	½	4
5300 ³	Birdman (IRE) *DavidSimcock* 2-8-12 MartinLane (6)	16 14/1	¾	5

2.25race Carmichael Humber 5ran 1m24.88   TF: 85, 83, 77, 76, 73 (-28)

Only a small field again for 2012's Champagne Stakes but it looks a stronger race than has perhaps tended to be the case recently, involving the winners of the Chesham (Tha'ir) and Acomb Stakes (Dundonnell), whilst Birdman and Maxentius both had placed form at this level already and Toronado had made a big impression with his 2 wins in a lower grade; it was the pair that dominated the betting that fought out a tight finish, Toronado and Dundonnell evidently very closely matched, a slight tactical advantage for the first-named (made all) making the difference between them on the day. **Toronado**'s impressive debut win had an even stronger look to it coming into this race than it had when we last saw him, the placed pair from Newbury both having improved a lot in the interim (Ayaar, who finished third, had won a German Group 3), and he kept up his unbeaten start with a smart effort up further in grade; that he made the running in a small field like this was a bit of an advantage, unpressured in front, quickening as suited him and getting first run on Dundonnell, but he's not flattered, the runner-up still having his chance to get by, and the determination shown by Toronado to fend off a strong challenge will continue to serve him well, whilst being involved in a tougher finish like this could also aid his development; the Racing Post Trophy back here at the end of next month is a likely target and, with the step up to 1m expected to suit, he remains open to improvement, whilst looking ahead to next year his physique suggests he's the type to train on well. **Dundonnell** could have beaten Toronado under slightly different circumstances, not having the run of the race to the same extent as that rival, so he did well under the circumstances and deserves credit for being the only one to get in a serious blow, upholding all of the positives that came out of his Acomb win, and like the winner he remains with the potential to improve, especially as a 3-y-o given his size and strength; he was held on to in third position until making smooth progress over 2f out, throwing down a challenge and holding every chance 1f out, and even though unable to get by the front-runner he stuck to his task to beat the rest comfortably. **Tha'ir** is proving consistent and likeable at a high level but is no longer really progressing and is vulnerable to smart juveniles like the first 2, beaten on merit here; chased leader, pushed along over 2f out, hung right, one paced; his best chance of further success will come at a lower level than this. **Maxentius** isn't quite up to this grade but at least bounced back to form after flopping at Goodwood 6 weeks earlier; held up, driven over 2f out, plugged on without threatening; not for the first time he was on edge in the preliminaries and he strikes as the sort to benefit from being gelded. **Birdman** had his limitations exposed under ideal conditions in the Futurity on his previous outing and, although not disgraced here, he essentially just found it a bit too competitive; held up, raced freely, headway halfway, pushed along over 2f out, weakened over 1f out.

CURRAGH Saturday, Sep 15
GOOD to SOFT

5923 Goffs Vincent O'Brien Stks (National)   7f
(Gr 1) (2yo c+f) £92,063

3048*	DAWN APPROACH (IRE) *JSBolger* 2-9-3 KJManning (2) 2/5f	1
5188²	DESIGNS ON ROME (IRE) *PatrickJFlynn* 2-9-3 DMGrant (7) 28/1 4¾	2
5729*	LEITIR MOR (IRE) *JSBolger* 2-9-3 (s+t) RPWhelan (5) 12/1 4¼	3
4794*	Probably (IRE) *DavidWachman* 2-9-3 WMLordan (1).............. 12/1 1½	4
5418*	Ayaar (IRE) *MickChannon,GB* 2-9-3 MHarley (4) 20/1 2	5
3962*	Nevis (IRE) *AidanO'Brien* 2-9-3 JosephO'Brien (3) 9/2 1¼	6
5300²	Flying The Flag (IRE) *AidanO'Brien* 2-9-3 SeamieHeffernan (6)... 12/1 ¾	7

6.40race Godolphin 7ran 1m25.50

There was little strength in depth in this latest renewal of the top 2-y-o race for colts in Ireland, the runner-up having been beaten off a mark of 89 in a nursery last time, and it proved to be a straightforward task for the odds-on favourite; Flying The Flag was ignored as he set a scorching pace. **Dawn Approach**, after 12 weeks off and over this 1f longer trip, maintained his unbeaten record to confirm that he is the best 2-y-o seen out this year, rounding off a fantastic day for Godolphin, in whose colours he was running for the first time; mid-field, pushed along soon after halfway, took time to hit full stride, led entering final 1f, wandered, driven out to win convincingly; the Dewhurst, a race which Jim Bolger has also targeted with his other winners of this race, namely Teofilo and New Approach (this one's sire) is reportedly next up, and, while he will be the one to beat there, it should tell us more about his classic credentials. **Designs On Rome** showed much improved form, fully justifiying connections decision to pitch him into this company, but things will be much tougher for him from here on in and it remains to be seen if he can back this up; held up, no match for winner, never nearer, flattered by proximity; will stay 1m. **Leitir Mor** is more exposed than the rest and ran respectably just 6 days after breaking his duck in a Group 3 here; chased leader, driven 3f out, challenged over 1f out, brushed aside by winner soon after and lost second close home. **Probably** fared no better than last time; held up, effort over 2f out, drifted right, made no impression; something to prove at present. **Ayaar** came into this on the back of a Group 3 win in Germany but was found out in better company; held up, off the bridle before most, never landed a blow. **Nevis**, who Joseph O'Brien switched on to after the withdrawal of Cristoforo Colombo, is bred in the purple but his form last time isn't working out, and he proved to be a major disappointment; held up, driven 3f out, made no impression, not persevered with once held; it is probably too soon to write him off but he clearly isn't one of his yard's leading lights. **Flying The Flag** run is best ignored; acted as pacemaker, soon well clear, headed entering final 1f, weakened; he has more scope than most of these and there are more races to be won with him back at a more realistic level.

NEWMARKET Friday, Sep 28
GOOD (Rowley Mile Course)

6268 Shadwell Fillies' Mile (Gr 1) (1) (2yo f)   1m

5851 *	CERTIFY (USA) MahmoodAlZarooni 2-8-12 MickaelBarzalona (2)	4/6f		1
4185 *	ROZ HarryDunlop 2-8-12 JimCrowley (5)	8/1	4½	2
5236 ³	AMAZONAS (IRE) EdDunlop 2-8-12 FrankieDettori (7)	12 10/1	1	3
5851 ⁵	Masarah (IRE) CliveBrittain 2-8-12 TomQueally (4)	100/1	hd	4
5061	Discernable MarkJohnston 2-8-12 SilvestreDeSousa (3)	14 11/1	¾	5
5236 ¹	Ollie Olga (USA) MickChannon 2-8-12 MartinHarley (6)	7/2	½	6

2.55race Godolphin 6ran 1m38.19   TF: 81, 70, 67, 67, 65, 64 (-32)

As Group 1 races go there's little depth to this year's Fillies' Mile, Certify proving to be in a different league, the rest finishing in a heap, amongst them Masarah, who looks to have been flattered after setting an ordinary gallop. **Certify** is the standard-setting juvenile filly at this point, stretching her unbeaten run to 4 now, but not actually having to improve much at all on her strong May Hill form, not having a smart rival like Purr Along to beat on this occasion, but she got the job done with real authority; she was waited with and travelled strongly towards the far side of the group, making smooth progress after 3f out and then quickening to lead around the 2f pole, soon clear and winning readily despite hanging left towards the centre of the track; this elevates her to clear favourite for next year's 1000 Guineas, understandably so with no doubting that she has the best form, but the level that she's at right now isn't good enough to win an average Guineas and there is reason to be concerned as to whether she'll train on and find the necessary improvement next year, firstly because she doesn't have a lot of size and scope, whilst her pedigree also suggested that she'd be precocious, a half-sister to Cry And Catch Me who was a Grade 1 winning 2-y-o in the US (disappointed on only subsequent run after her juvenile season). **Roz**'s Sandown listed win has proved strong form, the May Hill runner-up Purr Along one of those behind that day, and she improved a bit more up in grade and over this 1f longer trip; tracked pace, ridden 2f out, stuck to task; there's not obviously more to come from her at this stage but she seems straightforward and will continue to run well. **Amazonas** had no problem with this 1f longer trip as anticipated and again ran well, albeit in a substandard Group 1, and the feeling is that this is close to her limit; held up, not settle fully, headway 2f out, kept on. **Masarah** isn't up to this grade and is flattered by her proximity; made running, headed around 2f out, one paced, had the run of the race; achievement not all it might seem. **Discernable** returned to form 6 weeks after flopping in France but was beaten on merit and her development has stalled for now; in touch, raced freely, effort 3f out, not quicken; she does at least have physical scope. **Ollie Olga** was unbeaten to this point and had subsequent Moyglare winner Sky Lantern behind her in the Prestige, but she failed to meet expectations, possibly unsuited by the track; in touch, effort 3f out, hung right soon after (appeared not to handle the Dip), kept on under a hands-and-heels ride; worth another chance.

NEWMARKET Saturday, Sep 29
GOOD (Rowley Mile Course)

6303 Juddmonte Royal Lodge Stks (Gr 2) (1)   1m
(2yo c+g) £56,710

5559 *	STEELER (IRE) MarkJohnston 2-8-12 KieronFallon (5)	11/4		1
4369 ²	ARTIGIANO (USA) MahmoodAlZarooni 2-8-12 FrankieDettori (1)	8 7/1	1	2
5682 ²	AL WAAB (IRE) SirHenryCecil 2-8-12 TomQueally (9)	9/2 4/1	3½	3
5894 ⁵	Birdman (IRE) DavidSimcock 2-8-12 MartinLane (6)	22/1	ns	4
5496 *	Fantastic Moon JeremyNoseda 2-8-12 JohnnyMurtagh (7)	5/2 9/4f	½	5
5852 ³	One Word More (IRE) CharlesHills 2-8-12 WilliamCarson (2)	33/1	2¾	6
5019 ²	Excess Knowledge JohnGosden 2-8-12 WilliamBuick (4)	15/2 8/1	4	7
5496 ⁴	Mocenigo (IRE) PeterChapple-Hyam 2-8-12 RobertHavlin (8)	33/1	2	8

1.55race Sheikh Hamdan Bin Mohammed Al Maktoum 8ran 1m35.67

TF: 100, 98, 89, 89, 88, 81 (-15)

Generally the Royal Lodge isn't one of the deeper juvenile group races, with most of the top 2-y-o's being aimed at the Group 1s this autumn, but it's prestigious in its own right and usually produces a smart, progressive winner, Steeler fitting that bill here; it may have been a bit of an advantage to be prominent even though Birdman set a fair pace. **Steeler** benefited from this 1f longer trip as expected and improved a lot to get off the mark in group company, producing a smart performance, and it puts him in the mix as a classic contender for next year, not so flashy as some but progressive in his own right, and he'll stay beyond 1m, a likeable, strong-galloping sort who is out of a Park Hill winner; this performance typifies him, seeming uncomplicated as he was always prominent, taking over around 3f out, pushed along soon after and responding generously to fully assert in the final 100 yards; he's open to further improvement, the Racing Post Trophy on his agenda next, and he's the type to make a better 3-y-o too, tall and useful-looking. **Artigiano** was suited by this 1f longer trip and improved again to pull clear with an even more progressive rival, showing smart form himself; raced far side, chased leader, challenged over 1f out, stuck to task even though unable to stay with Steeler; he's in the Racing Post Trophy and is entitled to take his place, though clearly he's vulnerable as far as winning is concerned when up against the top juveniles. **Al Waab** ran well up further in grade, showing a similar level of form as on his previous 2 outings, and he left the impression that he'd benefit from the emphasis being even more on stamina, likely to be suited by at least 1¼m, leaving some potential for his 3-y-o season; held up, progress 3f out, driven over 1f out, one paced. **Birdman** is a useful juvenile with some strong form, in the frame in 3 group races now, but he's no longer progressing and had every chance under a change of tactics here, going from the front having not settled on his previous start; made running, headed around 3f out,

one paced; probably needs dropping in class if he's to be winning again. **Fantastic Moon** had created a very good impression previously and was unlucky not to finish closer here, sure to have made the first 3 but for trouble in-running, and he wasn't starting from such a good position as Steeler and Artigiano in the first place; mid-field, effort 3f out, hampered around 2f out and lost momentum, stayed on and finished with running left; there was enough in this performance to underline that he should be suited by 1m, and he's worth another chance. **One Word More** wasn't disgraced over this 1f longer trip but needs no excuses and is beginning to look exposed; tracked pace, ridden 3f out, left behind over 1f out. **Excess Knowledge**'s improvement at Newbury came only in a small-field listed event and he appeared to just find this too competitive up further in grade; chased leaders, off bridle before most, weakened over 1f out; he is bred to stay middle distances and has the physique to make a better 3-y-o, so there remains some potential. **Mocenigo** probably isn't quite up to this level but is better judged on his fourth in the Solario Stakes for the time being, too keen waited with and then hampered around 2f out when making an effort, dropped away soon after and not persevered with; he should stay 1m.

6304	Jaguar Cars Cheveley Park Stks (Gr 1) (1) (2yo f)		6f
	£92,721		
5182*	ROSDHU QUEEN (IRE) *WilliamHaggas* 2-8-12		1
	JohnnyMurtagh (1).. 9/2 4/1		
5635*	WINNING EXPRESS (IRE) *EdMcMahon* 2-8-12		1 2
	FrannyNorton (2)... 11/2 13/2		
5780²	BAILEYS JUBILEE *MarkJohnston* 2-8-12 KieranFallon (12)........ 20/1	ns	3
5791²	Upward Spiral *TomDascombe* 2-8-12 WilliamBuick (10)....... 18 16/1	1¼	4
5932*	Jillnextdoor (IRE) *MickChannon* 2-8-12 MartinHarley (3)........ 66/1	ns	5
5732⁶	Sendmylovetorose *AndrewOliver,Ireland* 2-8-12	hd	6
	ColmO'Donoghue (11)... 11/1		
5848⁴	Ceiling Kitty *TomDascombe* 2-8-12 RichardKingscote (7)....... 11 14/1	nk	7
5635²	Jadanna (IRE) *JamesGiven* 2-8-12 GrahamLee (8)................. 33/1	nk	8
4247*	Maureen (IRE) *RichardHannon* 2-8-12 RichardHughes (4)....... 2/11	¾	9
5848⁵	Hoyam *MichaelBell* 2-8-12 MickaelBarzalona (9)................. 16/1	nk	10
5814*	The Gold Cheongsam (IRE) *JeremyNoseda* 2-8-12	½	11
	FrankieDettori (6)... 8 11/2		
2.25race Clipper Logistics 11ran 1m11.10		TF: 80, 77, 77, 72, 72, 72 (-27)	

An open renewal of the Cheveley Park but not a strong one, none of the field meeting the standards for the race beforehand, and a bunched finish suggests a low view of the bare form; it doesn't look a solid result, either, as it proved hard for those held up to get involved, whilst a few of them got in each others way at crucial points too; they also raced in 2 groups, with the first 2 and the fifth (seems to have shown big improvement) going far side and the rest staying down the middle. **Rosdhu Queen** took another step up in grade in her stride, maintaining her unbeaten record with another improved effort, and her overall profile is obviously very positive even though there was an opportunistic element to this Group 1 success, the race itself not strong for the grade, whilst she also had the run of the race, making just about all towards the far rail; led, went with enthusiasm, tackled 1f out, found extra and showed an excellent attitude, something that will always stand her in good stead; she remains with potential, though primarily with sprinting in mind, and there are big stamina doubts if she's aimed at the 1000 Guineas next spring, 7f likely to be a maximum. **Winning Express** confirmed the positive impressions of her 2 wins as she ran well up again in grade, showing some further improvement, and, although not one of those held up, she shaped as if a stronger gallop would probably have been in her favour; raced far side chasing Rosdhu Queen (in touch overall), effort around 2f out, took a while to pick up fully but kept going well and closing at the finish; she's bred for speed and, though likely to stay 7f, there are doubts about her getting 1m if the Guineas is the target. **Baileys Jubilee** has been kept busy all year, her form up and down as a result, but this was a good effort, her best yet in form terms in fact, and she perhaps deserves some extra credit

for faring best of those that raced central throughout; tracked pace, progress on outer after 2f out, challenged 1f out, faded last 50 yards; likely to prove best at sprint trips. **Upward Spiral** hadn't been seen to best effect at Doncaster and resumed her progress here, suited by a more positive ride, leading the group down the centre until around 2f out and one paced after being headed (also got carried right), finding this barely enough of a test; she will be suited by 7f+ and remains open to improvement with a view to going over longer trips next year. **Jillnextdoor** had looked pretty much exposed before this and is possibly flattered by her apparent improvement; raced far side (along with the first 2), in mid-field overall, ridden over 2f out, kept on, well positioned; she's unsure to repeat this form next time. **Sendmylovetorose** shaped better than the bare result; raced centre, waited with, pushed along over 2f out, stayed on, unsuited by the way the race developed; should stay at least 7f. **Ceiling Kitty** seems to have run just respectably up 1f in trip, though not seen to best effect; raced centre, held up, headway over 1f out, one paced, not ideally placed; she'll always prove best as a sprinter and, given how speedy and precocious she's been this year, there has to be some doubt as to how well she'll train on (she's also not very big). **Jadanna** ran creditably but was not quite up to the task; raced centre, chased leaders, weakened over 1f out. **Maureen**, after 9 weeks off, failed to meet expectations; raced centre, tracked pace, not settle fully without cover, already looked held when not clear run over 1f out, failed to quicken and wasn't persevered with once it was clear she was beaten; she'd created a good impression previously and is well worth another chance. **Hoyam** wasn't seen to best effect; raced centre, dropped out, pushed along over 2f out, made no impression, disadvantaged by the run of the race. **The Gold Cheongsam** is best not judged on this run, unlucky not to finish closer; raced centre, held up, progress after 2f out, hampered entering final 1f, kept on without being knocked about having been left poorly placed; remains with potential based on what's gone before.

LONGCHAMP Sunday, Oct 7
HEAVY

6525	Total Prix Marcel Boussac - Criterium Des Pouliches (Gr 1) (2yo f) £136,048		1m
5305	SILASOL (IRE) *CLaffon-Parias,France* 2-8-11 OlivierPeslier (4)	13/1	1
	TOPAZE BLANCHE (IRE) *CLaffon-Parias,France* 2-8-11 FrankieDettori (8)	83/10	hd 2
5555[*]	ALTERITE (FR) *Jean-ClaudeRouget,France* 2-8-11 ChristopheSoumillon (7)	6/1	hd 3
5781[5]	Flotilla (FR) *MDelzangles,France* 2-8-11 GregoryBenoist (1)	24/1	1¼ 4
5781[*]	Peace Burg (FR) *JHeloury,France* 2-8-11 IoritzMendizabal (3)	2/1f	sn 5
5781[4]	Meri Shika (FR) *JBertrandeBalanda,France* 2-8-11 ThierryJarnet (5)		¾ 6
3128[2]	Agent Allison *PeterChapple-Hyam,GB* 2-8-11 JamieSpencer (9)	47/1	2 7
5851[2]	Purr Along *WilliamMuir,GB* 2-8-11 MartinDwyer (2)	65/10	1¾ 8
5732	My Special J'S (USA) *JohnPatrickShanahan,Ireland* 2-8-11 TadghO'Shea (10)	3/1	nk 9
		17/1	

1.30race Wertheimer et Frere 9ran 1m44.62

Just an ordinary renewal of the top race in France for 2-y-o fillies; if the principals are to make an impact at this sort of level next year, it's likely to be at further, given their pedigrees and that conditions here put the emphasis on stamina; Carlos Laffon-Parias, whose afternoon was to get even better, had the first 2 here, the winner from the same family as Solemia. **Silasol** (by Monsun; dam, useful French/US 1m (including at 2 yrs)/8.5f winner Stormina, out of half-sister to Solemia, winner of the Prix de l'Arc de Triomphe for same connections later in the afternoon) was up in grade and improved again to follow up a C&D success in a minor event gained in similar fashion last month; she led, was shaken up 2f out and responded well to hold off the challengers in the final 1f, proving determined; she makes more appeal as a middle-distance filly next year, rather than at 1m, and there's

better to come from her at 3, her sire more or less a guarantee of that, her attitude a definite plus as well. **Topaze Blanche** (by Zamindar; first foal of a French 12.5f winner, herself half-sister to smart French winner up to 1¼m Varxi) up in grade, took a step forward herself but just found her stable-companion too strong; held up, she ran on strongly to challenge in the final 1f, just failing; she's likely to stay 1¼m next year and is still unexposed; she'd won a maiden at Chantilly and minor event at Saint-Cloud last month. **Alterite**, who had been supplemented, progressed again; in rear, she made good progress down the outer in the straight, challenging in the final 1f and keeping on; she should stay 1¼m in due course. **Agent Allison** wasn't disgraced after nearly 4 months off over this 2f longer trip; close up, she was unable to quicken over 1f out before fading inside the last; she should prove fully effective at 1m. **Purr Along** failed to meet expectations and is better judged on previous form with subsequent Fillies' Mile winner Certify after things went wrong from an early stage; slowly into stride, she couldn't find a clear run through from the rear over 1f out, unable to make any further impression; she was subsequently reported to be in season. **My Special J's** fared no better than in the Moyglare, prominent before weakening over 1f out.

6526	Prix Jean-Luc Lagardere (Grand Criterium) Sponsored By Al Emadi Enterprises (Gr 1) (2yo c+f) £158,722		7f
4369[*]	OLYMPIC GLORY (IRE) *RichardHannon,GB* 2-9-0 RichardHughes (6)	12/10f	1
5737[*]	WHAT A NAME (IRE) *MDelzangles,France* 2-8-11 ChristophePLemaire (7)	3/1	1¼ 2
5814[4]	INDIAN JADE *KevinRyan,GB* 2-9-0 JamieSpencer (5)	45/1	nk 3
5065	Snowday (FR) *CLaffon-Parias,France* 2-9-0 OlivierPeslier (1)	20/1	5 4
4798[*]	Pedro The Great (USA) *AidanO'Brien,Ireland* 2-9-0 JosephO'Brien (2)	4/1	½ 5
5894[4]	Maxentius (IRE) *PeterChapple-Hyam,GB* 2-9-0 WilliamBuick (4)	32/1	2½ 6
5737[2]	Avantage (FR) *MmePiaBrandt,France* 2-9-0 GregoryBenoist (9)	16/1	1¾ 7
5894[3]	Tha'ir (IRE) *SaeeddbinSuroor,GB* 2-9-0 FrankieDettori (8)	73/10	½ 8

2.05race HE Sheikh Joaan bin Hamad Al Thani 8ran 1m25.73

Most of these had been beaten more times than they'd won, which isn't a good sign for a Group 1 2-y-o contest, but the first 2 (each representing Qatari interests who sponsor the meeting) were exceptions, and were among a trio to pull clear of the rest; Avantage and Snowday ensured a good pace early on. **Olympic Glory**, after 10 weeks off, was already proven under similar conditions and ran his best race; waited with, he moved into third once in the clear over 1f out and ran on well for pressure to lead in the last ½f; he's come closer than any so far to spoiling Dawn Approach's unbeaten record and would be unbeaten himself but for that run in the Coventry; his stable has other 2000 Guineas contenders, and Olympic Glory may have the French version as his spring target. **What A Name**, on softer ground than previously, ran well without quickening in the same manner as she had on good ground in the La Rochette; held up, she made headway over 1f out before keeping on to snatch second; she should stay 1m next year and could yet prove smart, this form at least on a par with that shown by the Marcel Boussac principals. **Indian Jade** looked to face a stiff task in this grade, but he had been shaping as though this sort of test would suit him well and he duly showed much improved form; he chased the leaders before being pushed along to lead narrowly over 1f out, headed inside the final 1f and losing second only close home. **Pedro The Great** needed to progress again to figure here but failed to make much of an impact, held up before headway on the rail over 2f out, unable to quicken over 1f out; he should stay this far. **Maxentius**, twice behind Olympic Glory in the summer, never looked like faring any better this time, in rear and making little impression. **Tha'ir** wasn't far behind Olympic Glory at Goodwood and had run well since on firmer ground but finished well held in very different conditions here; mid-field, he weakened from over 1f out and seems best on less testing ground.

NEWMARKET Saturday, Oct 13
GOOD (Rowley Mile Course)

6658 Vision.ae Middle Park Stks (Gr 1) (1) (2yo c) £85,065   6f

5065¹	RECKLESS ABANDON *CliveCox* 2-8-12 GeraldMosse (2) 5/2 9/4jf	1
6125¹	MOOHAAJIM (IRE) *MarcoBotti* 2-8-12 AdamKirby (7) 5/2 9/4jf	nk 2
5273⁶	GALE FORCE TEN *AidanO'Brien,Ireland* 2-8-12 (s)	nk 3
	ColmO'Donoghue (6) 33/1	
4798	Cristoforo Colombo (USA) *AidanO'Brien,Ireland* 2-8-12	1¾ 4
	RyanMoore (9) 9/2	
5814⁵	Parliament Square (IRE) *AidanO'Brien,Ireland* 2-8-12 (s)	2¾ 5
	SeamieHeffernan (4) 14 18/1	
6493²	Hototo *KevinRyan* 2-8-12 FrankieDettori (8) 25 16/1	ns 6
6125²	Master of War *RichardHannon* 2-8-12 RichardHughes (3) 16 12/1	¾ 7
6281³	Wexford Opera (IRE) *JSBolger,Ireland* 2-8-12 (t) KJManning (1).. 50/1	1½ 8
5225¹	Blaine *KevinRyan* 2-8-12 JamieSpencer (5) 11/1	9 9
6125⁵	Heavy Metal *MarkJohnston* 2-8-12 JoeFanning (10) 25/1	3¼ 10

2.20race Miss J. Deadman & Mr S. Barrow 10ran 1m1.06
TF: 117, 117, 116, 110, 101, 101 (=)

Dream Ahead's top-class performance in this race in 2010 pushes up the recent standards somewhat and this is essentially a good, solid renewal of the Middle Park, featuring the winners of most of the big 2-y-o sprinting prizes up to this point, with Heavy Metal, Blaine, Moohaajim and Reckless Abandon all having won 6f pattern races previously; the pace was sound but, whilst there's no doubting the winner's performance, it's true to say that several performed well in making the running against the stand rail on the afternoon and there might have been a slight advantage there. **Reckless Abandon** has risen to every challenge thrown at him in 5 starts this year and firmed up his status as the best of the sprinting 2-y-os by completing the Prix Morny-Middle Park double, albeit with less to spare this time, and it could well be that he's performed close to his limit here, not least because he lacks the physical scope to be much better next year; the manner of this win was similar to Deauville, breaking fast to overcome a potentially problematic draw in stall 2, soon getting across to lead on the stand rail (a position that may have been an advantage considering how others on the day fared under similar tactics), going with plenty of enthusiasm and digging deep after Moohaajim tackled him around 1f out, showing a professional attitude; there were inevitably Guineas quotes afterwards but speed is his main attribute and he's always likely to prove best at sprint trips. **Moohaajim** couldn't quite turn the tables with Reckless Abandon from the Morny but got much closer, underlining the progress that he's made since, this his best performance yet, and he's taken to prove the best of these next season, not the biggest of colts by any means but having more strength and substance to him than the winner, and it could be argued that he deserves as much credit on the day, anyway, having started further back than the pair he split and not been against the stand rail like the winner; held up, travelled fluently, smooth progress after halfway, challenged 1f out and kept on without being able to get by; he obviously has a lot of speed, but he's bred to stretch to the Guineas trip and that will presumably be the aim in the spring. **Gale Force Ten** reportedly returned lame at the Curragh in August, so that run was easy to forgive, and he found improvement after 7 weeks off, finishing even closer to Reckless Abandon here than he had when runner-up in the Norfolk at Royal Ascot; raced wide, chased leaders, every chance over 1f out, stuck to his task, has the physique to train on, a tall and attractive colt, and will stay at least 7f. **Cristoforo Colombo** may well already be a Group 1 winner had he not slipped up in the Phoenix and boasts strong form prior to that, notably when third to Dawn Approach and Olympic Glory in the Coventry, and he shaped well here with a view to stepping up to 7f+, hitting the frame despite the test looking inadequate—he was soon behind and outpaced, began to make progress

after halfway and stayed on to be nearest at the finish; he'd be interesting if sent to America for the Breeders Cup next month (most likely in the Juvenile Turf), whilst it wouldn't be a huge surprise if he were to make an impact in the 2000 Guineas next year, an outsider to at least consider (currently available at 33/1). **Parliament Square** hasn't repeated his Prix Morny effort on either outing since, the form he showed that day seemingly his limit; raced off the pace, kept on but never a threat. **Hototo** wasn't disgraced just a week on from a good second in Redcar's 2-y-o Trophy, basically not quite up to the task in this grade, his limit already reached; close up, weakened approaching final 1f. **Master of War** had already started to look exposed and is unlikely to ever be up to Group 1 standard, but he underperformed here in any case; steadied at the start, in rear, progress after halfway, effort flattened out. **Wexford Opera** was flying too high in this grade; mid-field, off the bridle before most, faded over 1f out, never a threat. **Blaine** is better than this, proven by his Gimcrack win, and clearly wasn't 100% on the day; mid-field, went with little fluency, beaten 2f out and eased off. **Heavy Metal** ran one of his poorer races of the season and looks to have had enough for the year now; chased leaders, off the bridle before most, lost place approaching 2f out.

6659 Dubai Dewhurst Stks (Gr 1) (1) (2yo c+f) £170,130			7f
5923* DAWN APPROACH (IRE) *JSBolger,Ireland* 2-9-1			1
KJManning (3)		1/3 3/10f	
5923³ LEITIR MOR (IRE) *JSBolger,Ireland* 2-9-1 (s+t) RPWhelan (1) 33/1			2¾ 2
5729⁶ GEORGE VANCOUVER (USA) *AidanO'Brien,Ireland* 2-9-1			¾ 3
JosephO'Brien (6)		16/1	
5852* Ashdan *JohnGosden* 2-9-1 WilliamBuick (2)		9/2	4 4
4115* The Ferryman (IRE) *AidanO'Brien,Ireland* 2-9-1 RyanMoore (6) 12 14/1			2½ 5
6125 Funk Soul Brother *CharlesHills* 2-9-1 MichaelHills (5)		100/1	4 6
2.55race Godolphin 6ran 1m24.00		TF: 122, 115, 112, 101, 94, 82 (-4)	

The 2012 Dewhurst wasn't quite the defining 2-y-o race it has often been, lacking depth with no serious challenger to Dawn Approach, but the unbeaten winner has shown a high level of form, exceeded only by New Approach and Frankel in terms of ratings achieved by the winner of this race in the last 5 years; a sound pace was set by Leitir Mor, though he may have had an advantage in racing up against the stand rail, and George Vancouver probably deserves as much credit as the runner-up. **Dawn Approach** had a surprisingly simple opportunity given how competitive the Dewhurst has often been in recent years, facing only 5 rivals and well ahead of all of them on previous form, but in getting the job done he completed an excellent year, unbeaten in 6 races, including the Coventry Stakes and National Stakes before this, and, although the ratings he's achieved are a little way short of some other recent top 2-y-os, at this stage Dawn Approach is the highest-rated juvenile of 2012; he's never been a flashy, strong-travelling sort and the style of this latest win was familiar, chasing the leaders and pushed along with more than 2f left, then responding well on leaving the Dip, taking over from his front-running stablemate under 1f out and well on top at the finish; there's no question that stepping up to 1m for the 2000 Guineas will suit Dawn Approach—it's exactly this that leaves him with the potential to achieve more—and he will be a big player back at Newmarket in May, for all there's plenty of time and opportunity yet for others to stake major claims; despite Godolphin's ownership, he will be staying in training with Jim Bolger, incidentally. **Leitir Mor** showed improved form to be second in a Group 1, much closer to Dawn Approach here than in Ireland last month, though he's possibly a bit flattered, making the running on the stand rail certainly not a disadvantage on the day as a whole, and he was no match for his stablemate once he

got to him under 1f out, keeping on to hold off the challenge of the third; this was his twelfth start of the season and he's clearly tough. **George Vancouver** had no obvious excuse when disappointing in a Group 3 last month but wasted no time getting back on track, confirming the form he showed when second in the Morny; held up, switched over 2f out, headway out wide soon after, one paced, probably wasn't ideally placed as it panned out and can be given a little extra credit; he's a smart juvenile, though not one of his yard's leading lights, and he doesn't have a great deal of physical scope. **Ashdan** had created a good impression with wins at a lower level but failed to meet expectations up in grade, seeming just to find it too competitive; held up, headway under pressure 2f out, weakened final 1f; will stay 1m+ and is a good sort physically, so although this dents his profile and potential it's too early to write him off. **The Ferryman** found it too competitive jumping straight from a maiden win 11 weeks ago into Group 1 company, weakening over 1f out having chased the leader; he is a big, rangy colt with plenty of scope and could easily make into a better 3-y-o with this in mind. **Funk Soul Brother** was flying too high in this grade; mid-field, not settle fully, struggling over 2f out, weakened over 1f out; needs dropping in class.

6661 **Vision.ae Rockfel Stks (Gr 2) (1) (2yo f)** £34,026   7f

5019° JUST THE JUDGE (IRE) *CharlesHills* 2-8-12 MichaelHills (3) 11/2 6/1	1
5812² NARGYS (IRE) *LucaCumani* 2-8-12 KierenFallon (9) 6 5/1 1¾ 2
5676³ DESERT BLOSSOM (IRE) *MahmoodAlZarooni* 2-8-12	1 3
MichaelBarzalona (4) 11 12/1	
6109° Melody of Love *AnnDuffield* 2-8-12 FrankieDettori (1) .... 8 15/2 ¾ 4
6109³ Momalorka *WilliamHaggas* 2-8-12 (s) KellyHarrison (2) .... 50/1 hd 5
6176° Zurigha (IRE) *RichardHannon* 2-8-12 RichardHughes (6) 16 14/1 1 6
5732² Scintillula (IRE) *JSBolger,Ireland* 2-8-12 (s) KJManning (5) .... 4 5/1 ½ 7
6189° Gift From Heaven (IRE) *DavidWachman,Ireland* 2-8-12 .... nk 8
WMLordan (11) 4 11/4f	
5851° Go Angellica (IRE) *DavidSimcock* 2-8-12 WilliamBuick (8) 25/1 2¼ 9
6265³ Annie's Fortune (IRE) *AlanJarvis* 2-8-12 JimCrowley (10) 9 11/1 1½ 10
6268⁴ Masarah (IRE) *CliveBrittain* 2-8-12 TomQueally (7) .... 28/1 ½ 11
4.05race Qatar Racing Limited & Sangster Family 11ran 1m25.15	

TF: 99, 94, 91, 89, 88, 85 (-6)

It might be an ordinary year for juvenile fillies in general but this looks a pretty good renewal of the Rockfel, at least with regards to the first 2, both of whom are progressing well; the pace was fair but they bunched up towards the stand rail and a few got in each others way as things were taking shape, Nargys the worst affected. **Just The Judge** has got better with each start so far, improving again to maintain her unbeaten record up further in grade, showing near-smart form and doing it impressively, albeit having got first run on one that was denied a run at a crucial stage; mid-field, travelled well, quickened to lead over 1f out, kept going well; this throws her right into the 1000 Guineas picture, amongst the best juvenile fillies now, and she remains open to improvement, a lengthy, attractive filly who looks sure to be suited by 1m. **Nargys** is most progressive, an excellent second in a competitive nursery last month, and she more than coped up in grade, improving again on the face of it and unlucky not to at least finish closer to the winner, sure to have given her plenty to think about if she'd got a clear run; tracked pace, travelled as well as any, denied a run 2f out until 1f out, finished well but had conceded first run once in the clear; likely to stay 1m, is quite an imposing sort and may do better still. **Desert Blossom** ran her best race yet and wasn't seen to very best effect, either; in rear, forced very wide around 2f out, progress over 1f out, kept on, not ideally placed; still unexposed. **Melody of Love** didn't improve any further on her Firth of Clyde win but again ran well over this 1f longer trip, more or less backing up the improvement that she'd shown there; held up, headway under pressure over 2f out, one paced; likeable filly, will continue to give a good account. **Momalorka**, back up in trip, showed improved form; waited with, headway over 2f out, kept on; this was a good effort but she's not going to be the easiest to place. **Zurigha** was fast-tracked to group company by her powerful yard only 19 days after winning a maiden, in itself telling something of the regard that she's held in, and she took a step forward in form terms without quite being up to the task; close up, every chance 2f out, weakened final 1f; this should help her development and she remains open to improvement. **Scintillula** was easy to back and failed to confirm previous form, not quickening having raced prominently and beaten 1f out; worth another chance. **Gift From Heaven**'s impressive debut came in the mud and, though not discredited up in grade, it would be fair to say that she didn't live up to expectations given how well backed she was; mid-field, went with little fluency, never a threat; not one to be writing off yet. **Go Angellica** disappointed for the second start in a row, and her development looks to have stalled; steadied at the start, never landed a blow. **Annie's Fortune** ran one of the poorer races of her season; raced stand side, led, joined around 2f out, weakened. **Masarah** was flattered in the Fillies Mile and was essentially out of her depth here; chased leaders, no room 2f out, dropped away soon after.

6662 Autumn Stks (Gr 3) (1) (2yo) £22,684   1m

0155*	TRADING LEATHER (IRE) *JSBolger,Ireland* 2-9-0 KJManning (4)	5/2jf		1
6024*	MONTIRIDGE (IRE) *RichardHannon* 2-9-0 RichardHughes (8)	5/2jf	¾	2
5759*	EYE OF THE STORM (IRE) *AidanO'Brien,Ireland* 2-9-0 JosephO'Brien (2)	9 7/1	3	3
5898⁴	Glory Awaits (IRE) *KevinRyan* 2-9-0 JamieSpencer (10)	40/1	1¼	4
4952*	Galileo Rock (IRE) *DavidWachman,Ireland* 2-9-0 WMLordan (7)	6 11/2	nk	5
5632*	Cap O'Rushes *MahmoodAlZarooni* 2-9-0 FrankieDettori (9)	12 10/1	ns	6
5856*	Flying Officer (USA) *JohnGosden* 2-9-0 (h) WilliamBuick (1)	10 11/1	3½	7
5682⁵	Makafeh *LucaCumani* 2-9-0 KierenFallon (11)	33/1	½	8
6408²	King Dragon (IRE) *BrianMeehan* 2-9-0 RyanMoore (6)	40/1	3½	9
5816*	Glenard *CharlesHills* 2-9-0 MichaelHills (5)	20/1	6	10
6452*	Pinarius (IRE) *BrianMeehan* 2-9-0 (v) MartinLane (3)	100/1	nk	11

4.40race Mrs J. S. Bolger 11ran 1m37.83   TF: 104, 102, 95, 92, 91, 91 (-7)

More than half of this year's Autumn Stakes field arrived unbeaten, so there was plenty of potential amongst them, and the pair that headed the betting stepped up to the mark, pulling clear of the remainder, Trading Leather's performance as good as any winner of this race since Kite Wood took it in 2008; the pace was steady for the first 1f or so before Glory Awaits upped the tempo. **Trading Leather** had made a promising start before this, second only to the very talented Battle of Marengo on his debut prior to an easy maiden win, and he followed that up with a Group 3 success on just his third career outing, showing a smart level of form; prominent, led over 1f out, tackled by the strong-travelling Montiridge soon after but battled well and showed a really good attitude; will be suited by further than 1m and remains open to improvement. **Montiridge** ran well over this 1f longer trip and up in grade, improving on the form of his 2 wins, and he's worth as much credit as the winner given things didn't go as smoothly for him on the day; waited with and took a strong hold early on, headway when bumped over 2f out, continued to make smooth progress after and loomed up to challenge the winner around 1f out, faded late on as his early exertions appeared to take their toll; there are still things that he has to learn but he's in the best hands to fulfil his potential and remains open to improvement. **Eye of The Storm** ran well up in grade just 4 weeks after his impressive maiden win, shaping a bit better than the bare result; raced wide, dropped out, not clear run around 2f out, stayed on under hands and heels from a less-than-ideal position; a stoutly-bred colt, he will prove suited by middle distances as a 3-y-o and is capable of better still. **Glory Awaits** faced a stiff task in group company but gave a reasonable account, doing as well as could be expected; raced against stand rail and made running, went in snatches, headed over 1f out, one paced; a potentially lenient handicap mark is bound to suffer as a result of this, though.

Galileo Rock is stoutly bred and more testing conditions than this suited him on his debut, bringing stamina more into play, and although not disgraced up in grade the test seemed inadequate; chased leaders, outpaced over 2f out, unable to quicken; bred to be suited by 1½m+ and remains with potential for his 3-y-o campaign. **Cap O'Rushes** was found out in better company after 2 wins at a lower level; mid-field, driven 2f out, kept on, never a threat; will stay at least 1¼m. **Flying Officer** who was fitted with a hood and upped in grade on the back of his debut win, found this too competitive and still looked a little rough around the edges; held up, never on terms, not knocked about; he remains unexposed and may do better at a lower level with more time. **Makafeh** was basically out of his depth; in touch, weakened over 1f out, not persevered with once held. **King Dragon** is not up to this better company; raced off the pace, never landed a blow. **Glenard**'s debut form hasn't worked out so well as might have been expected and he struggled up in grade, held up and never on terms. **Pinarius** was flying too high in this grade; in touch, lost place 2f out.

DONCASTER Saturday, Oct 27
GOOD to SOFT

6982	Racing Post Trophy (Gr 1) (1) (2yo c+f) £122,494	1m (Str.)

6602 ³	KINGSBARNS (IRE) AidanO'Brien,Ireland 2-9-0		
	JosephO'Brien (7)	9/4 15/8f	1
6731 ³	VAN DER NEER RichardHannon 2-9-0 RichardHughes (1)	9/2 5/1	1¾ 2
6303 ⁴	STEELER (IRE) MarkJohnston 2-9-0 KierenFallon (3)	7/2	sh 3
5300 ⁴	First Cornerstone (IRE) AndrewOliver,Ireland 2-9-0		2 4
	ChrisHayes (4)	10 11/1	
6662 ⁷	Trading Leather (IRE) J.SBolger,Ireland 2-9-0 KJManning (5)	10/3 3/1	3½ 5
5137 ⁶	Sir Patrick Moore (FR) HarryDunlop 2-9-0 HayleyTurner (6)	50/1	6 6
6303 ⁴	Birdman (IRE) DavidSimcock 2-9-0 MartinLane (2)	50/1	7 7

3.05race Mrs John Magnier,Mr M.Tabor & Mr D.Smith 7ran 1m40.32
TF: 116, 111, 111, 106, 97, 82 (-4)

Often one of the most significant 2-y-o races of the season, won by several subsequent classic winners, and, although this year as a whole isn't a particularly strong one for juveniles, the form shown by the unexposed Kingsbarns here is bettered only by Crowded House (2008) and St Nicholas Abbey (2009) in the previous 5 renewals of this, and there were 3 Group winners in behind in Steeler, First Cornerstone and Trading Leather; the gallop was fair and it is a solid result. **Kingsbarns** arrived with potential that far exceeded his achievement, only having won a weak maiden 17 days earlier, but that Ballydoyle thought him worthy of his place at Group 1 level (had to be supplemented for this) said plenty in itself and he duly proved himself to be the real deal, comfortably seeing off some smart opponents with a bare performance that's about on par with the recent standards for Racing Post Trophy winners, and he's value for more on top as well; it was a smooth all-round display, never really a moment's worry as Kingsbarns tracked the pace travelling strongly, and once produced to lead under 2f out he was immediately in control, drifting left slightly in the final 1f but ridden out to essentially win readily; as with his stablemate Camelot last year, who also won this race on only his second start, there's no doubt that Kingsbarns will stay middle distances and probably be better for them, an obvious Derby candidate at this stage, but he showed a high enough cruising speed here to also put him in the mix for the 2000 Guineas in the spring should connections decide to go down that route, likely to end the year with only Dawn Approach ahead of him in the 2-y-o colt rankings, and clearly he has further potential, not only very lightly raced but most imposing physically, a rangy, attractive colt who should certainly make into an even better 3-y-o. **Van Der Neer** justified connections' decision to supplement him earlier in the week, losing his unbeaten record but still taking his form

to a different level behind a potentially top-class opponent in Kingsbarns; held up, progress after halfway, hung right over 1f out, stuck to his task without being a match for the winner. **Steeler** (edgy/on toes in prelims) has proven himself a smart, tough juvenile and ran well on softer ground than previously, more or less confirming the improvement that he'd shown to win the Royal Lodge; chased leader, led 3f out, headed under 2f out, kept on even though caught for second on the post; he'll stay further than 1m and, although it seems unlikely that he'll be good enough for the top races next year, he should continue to be competitive at group level; his trainer indicated that he's likely to join Godolphin. **First Cornerstone**'s Futurity win is easy to pick holes in and it's no real surprise that he was unable to find the improvement it would have taken to have a say in this much stronger contest, running creditably but just not quite up to the task; tracked pace, progress 3f out to almost be on terms, driven over 1f out and one paced; bred to stay beyond 1m. **Trading Leather** failed to meet expectations on the back of his Autumn Stakes win, possibly finding the softer ground against him, whilst there's also a chance that this came too soon after what was a fairly hard race at Newmarket; led, headed 3f out, weakened 2f out; he's shown that he's better than this and hasn't necessarily shown all that he has to offer yet, still to try beyond 1m after all. **Sir Patrick Moore** was flying too high in this grade, and is better judged on previous form; held up, raced freely, made no impression. **Birdman** is more exposed than the rest and was basically out of his depth; dwelt, always behind.

NEWBURY Saturday, Oct 27
HEAVY

6988 Worthington's Whizz-Kidz Stks (Horris Hill)   7f
(Gr 3) (1) (2yo c+g) £20,983

6770 ¹	TAWHID *SaeedbinSuroor* 2-8-12 JimCrowley (2)	5 9/2	1
5065	ALHEBAYEB (IRE) *RichardHannon* 2o-9-3 PaulHanagan (7)	5/1	4 2
6158 ¹	BOOMSHACKERLACKER (IRE) *GeorgeBaker* 2-8-12	1¾ 3
	PatCosgrave (1)	8 9/1
6457 ¹	Half A Person (IRE) *PeterChapple-Hyam* 2-8-12	½ 4
	JamieSpencer (5)	9 8/1
6674 ²	Odooj (IRE) *WilliamHaggas* 2-8-12 DaneO'Neill (4)	5 9/2	2½ 5
6232 ³	Glean *RichardHannon* 2-8-12 RyanMoore (6)	9/2 7/2f	3 6
6526 ⁶	Maxentius (IRE) *PeterChapple-Hyam* 2-8-12 WilliamBuick (8)	6 13/2	6 7
5693 ⁴	Hasopop (IRE) *MarcoBotti* 2-8-12 AdamKirby (3)	14/1	¾ 8

2.15race Godolphin 8ran 1m29.64   TF: 113, 107, 97, 95, 88, 80 (=)

A few of the more established performers failed to give their running but it was hard not to be impressed by the winner, who is developing well physically and was clearly much improved up in grade, his performance the best in this race in recent years. **Tawhid** attracted support upped in grade and stepped up markedly on the form he'd shown in maidens, proving most progressive; waited with, travelled strongly, led over 1f out, quickened clear, impressive; one to keep on side and presumably will have something like the Greenham on the agenda next spring. **Alhebayeb** ran creditably after 9 weeks off over this 1f longer trip; disputed lead, led over 2f out, headed 1f out, no match for winner; likely to prove best up to 7f; probably won't be the easiest to place at 3 yrs. **Boomshackerlacker** with a better chance than the market suggested, was below form after 5 weeks off, the slightly longer trip on testing ground perhaps stretching him; handy, challenged 2f out, no extra 1f out; likely to prove best up to easy 7f. **Half A Person** ran about as well as could have been expected upped in grade, though never getting on terms with the principals; slowly into stride, held up, effort 2f out, kept on; remains with potential and worth a try at 1m. **Odooj**, the subject of market support, was below form, beaten by more than this 1f longer trip on ground that he was proven on; held up, never landed a blow;

should stay 7f. **Glean**, on softer ground than previously, was below form; tracked pace, pushed along over 2f out, soon beaten; type to resume progress away from testing ground. **Maxentius** was below form, even in lesser pattern company, his efforts since his 2 wins suggesting firmly that he's just not quite up to the grade he's running in; disputed lead, took keen hold, weakened 2f out, eased off. **Hasopop** ran poorly after 7 weeks off, a lack of stamina a possible explanation for his effort, given he'd shown his best form on similarly testing ground, though over 6f; tracked pace, not settle fully, ridden and hung right over 2f out, soon beaten.

LEOPARDSTOWN Saturday, Oct 27
SOFT

7003 JRA Killavullan Stks (Gr 3) (2yo) £25,102   7f

5713 ¹	BIG BREAK *DKWeld* 2-9-0 PatSmullen (3)	10/11f	1
6857 ⁵	BEYOND THANKFUL (IRE) *JSBolger* 2-9-3 RPWhelan (7)	10/1	3¾ 2
6727 ¹	COOLIBAH (IRE) *CharlesO'Brien* 2-9-0 DeclanMcDonagh (6)	20/1	1 3
6232 ⁶	Canary Row (IRE) *PJPrendergast* 2-9-3 ShaneFoley (5)	14/1	sh 4
5496 ⁶	Dont Bother Me (IRE) *NiallMoran* 2-9-3 WMLordan (2)	12/1	2 5
6603 ¹	Dubaya *AndrewOliver* 2-9-0 GFCarroll (8)	7/1	½ 6
6686 ¹	Magician (IRE) *AidanO'Brien* 2-9-3 SeamieHeffernan (4)	15/8	9 7

2.40race Mr K. Abdulla 7ran 1m32.68

Not a great renewal of this Group 3 on the whole, but take nothing away from the winner who produced a smart performance and is a potential classic filly next term; the pace was ordinary. **Big Break**, who was strong in betting, coped well with the step up in grade, is most progressive and is one to keep onside next season, very possibly at the highest level; tracked pace, travelled strongly, forced to switch early in straight, quickened to lead entering final 1f, went clear late on, impressive; a full sister to the stable's Famous Name, she promises to stay at least a mile and is capable of better still. **Beyond Thankful** who's being kept busy, resumed progress; mid-field, avoided the trouble down the inner when making his effort over 1f out, kept on, no match for winner; not easy to place. **Coolibah** ran well upped in grade and has improved with each run; slowly into stride, held up, ridden entering straight, best work finish; will prove suited by at least 1¼m. **Canary Row** ran creditably and has seemingly reached his limit in form terms; close up, challenged early in straight, led briefly over 1f out, slightly hampered, one paced. **Dont Bother Me** ran up to his best, and is no longer progressing; made running, headed before halfway, led again entering straight, weakened before final 1f; probably needs dropping in class. **Dubaya** found this too competitive, and ran to a similar level as on debut; waited with, driven approaching home turn, made little impression. **Magician** is better judged on his previous form; close up, led before halfway, headed entering straight, disputing for the lead under pressure when badly hampered under 2f out, heavily eased off.

SAINT-CLOUD Thursday, Nov 1
HEAVY

7099	Criterium International (Gr 1) (2yo c+f) £115,202		1m
6922 ²	LOCH GARMAN (IRE) *JSBolger,Ireland* 2-9-0 KJManning	55/10	1
6484 ⁴	ANNA'S PEARL *RalphBeckett,GB* 2-9-0 (v) JimCrowley	13/1	½ 2
6623 ⁴	US LAW (IRE) *PBary,France* 2-9-0 ChristopheSoumillon	3/1	1¼ 3
	Triple Threat (FR) *AFabre,France* 2-9-0 MaximeGuyon	15/10f	3½ 4
6623 ²	Kenhope (FR) *H-APantall,France* 2-8-11 OlivierPeslier	65/10	4 5
6699 ³	Pearl Flute (IRE) *FHGraffard,France* 2-9-0 JohnnyMurtagh	55/10	7 6

Mrs J. S. Bolger 6ran 1m52.70

Won last year by subsequent 2000 Guineas runner-up French Fifteen (and by Irish 2000 Guineas winner Roderic O'Connor in 2010), this hardly looked a Group 1 line-up beforehand, Pearl Flute (ran no sort of race in this ground) and US Law (not settle/found little) setting the standard as Group 3 winners but not raising the bar very high, and it was fought out instead by the pair with the most to do on form, the runner-up still a maiden and the winner barely a week on from his debut; that said, Loch Garman looks another interesting prospect from the stable of the season's leading 2-y-o Dawn Approach; more was clearly expected of Andre Fabre's representative Triple Threat after an easy C&D win last time but he was under pressure from the home turn. **Loch Garman** improved plenty to become a Group 1 winner just 8 days after his debut, and while he'd known his job up against other newcomers last week, the overriding impression he gave here was that he's not yet the finished article; patiently ridden after initially breaking well, he was pushed along with only one behind him before the home turn and still had a bit to do when driven 2f out, but made relentless headway under pressure in the straight, staying on to lead close home as the leader tired, responding well and showing a good attitude; he's one to be interested in for next year, and though recent winners of this race have gone on to perform well in a Guineas at 3, and his family is essentially a speedy one, he gave the strong impression here that he'll prove suited by further than 1m in due course; physically, he looks to have scope for plenty of improvement. **Anna's Pearl**, in a first-time visor over this 1f longer trip, faced an apparently stiff task in this grade but showed much improved form in going close; he made the running, was shaken up 2f out and still had a clear advantage entering the final 1f but was tiring when headed close home; he'd be a banker for a maiden somewhere along the line, though this will have encouraged connections to keep his sights pretty high; a testing 1m is likely to prove his limit stamina-wise.

SANTA ANITA Friday, Nov 2
FIRM

7142 Breeders' Cup Juv Fillies Turf (Gr 1) (2yo f) £335,404 1m

6525[4]	FLOTILLA (FR) *MDelzangles,France* 2-8-10	ChristophePLemaire (4)	114/10		1
1580*	WATSDACHANCES (IRE) *ChadCBrown,USA* 2-8-10	JavierCastellano (6)	6/1	1¼	2
5941	SUMMER OF FUN (USA) *GeorgeWeaver,USA* 2-8-10	RamonADominguez (2)	43/1	½	3
6509[4]	Tara From The Cape (USA) *ToddAPletcher,USA* 2-8-10	JohnRVelazquez (8)	148/10	1	4
6483[3]	The Gold Cheongsam (IRE) *JeremyNoseda,GB* 2-8-10 (b)	WilliamBuick (12)	27/1	hd	5
6265*	Waterway Run (USA) *RalphBeckett,GB* 2-8-10	FrankieDettori (10)	106/10	1	6
	Moonwalk (USA) *DaleLRomans,USA* 2-8-10	CoreyJLanerie (11)	38/1	¾	7
5732*	Sky Lantern (IRE) *RichardHannon,GB* 2-8-10	RichardHughes (3)	27/10f	¾	8
6511	Nancy O (IRE) *CarolynMCostigan,Canada* 2-8-3	DavidMoran[7] (9)	41/1	hd	9
6648[4]	Infanta Branca (USA) *AidanO'Brien,Ireland* 2-8-10	RyanMoore (15)	42/1	nk	10
	Flashy Ways (USA) *RBaltas,USA* 2-8-10 (b)	JosephTalamo (13)	77/10	½	11
	Kitten's Point (USA) *HGrahamMotion,USA* 2-8-10	RafaelBejarano (1)	161/10	½	12
5941*	Spring Venture (USA) *MarkECasse,Canada* 2-8-10 (b)	PatrickHusbands (5)	7/2	½	13
	Oscar Party (USA) *WayneMCatalano,USA* 2-8-10	KentJDesormeaux (7)	47/1	½	14

9.28race Sheikh Mohammed bin Khalifa Al Thani 14ran 1m34.64

The winner's performance, particularly the turn of foot 1f out, was impressive, but otherwise this result isn't particularly satisfactory with several horses running into each other coming off the sharp bend into the straight; the favourite Sky Lantern looked a big player before she was denied any sort of run, and is the most likely one to make into a genuine Group 1 performer next year. **Flotilla** has been progressive all year, but took a much more marked step up to take this in good style; mid-field, travelled strongly, shaken up early in straight, quickened impressively to lead final 1f, had bit in hand; will stay 1¼m next year, when she may well do better still. **Watsdachances** produced another big effort but had no excuses whatsoever and lacks the scope of some of those around her; mid-field, steady headway 2f out, every chance 1f out, stuck to task; should remain competitive in pattern company, but likely to prove vulnerable at the top level from hereonin. **Summer of Fun** found the improvement required to get competitive and could arguably be marked up a little; raced off the pace, denied a run early in straight, kept going well without jockey going for everything when clearly set for third. **The Gold Cheongsam** continued her progress in first-time blinkers, leaving the impression there may be even more to come from her as a 3-y-o, too; patiently ridden, took time to knuckle down, finished best by some way; will stay 1¼m next year. **Waterway Run** ran creditably stepping up in grade, but had no excuses; close up, travelled smoothly, briefly short of a run after 2f out, but failed to quicken once in the clear; could get back on the up with her sights lowered. **Sky Lantern** deserved to be sent off favourite given what she'd achieved previously and would surely have gone a long way to justifying it with a clear run; mid-field, travelled smoothly, made good, threatening progress on home turn, but never able to open up fully in straight and finished with plenty of running left as jockey eased down; all her potential remains in tact and the Guineas is presumably the next big race on her agenda. **Infanta Branca** was basically out of her depth but far from discredited on the figures; dropped out, never landed a blow from a long way back.

SANTA ANITA Saturday, Nov 3
FIRM

7150 Breeders' Cup Juv Turf (Gr 1) (2yo c+g) £215,045 1m

6659[3]	GEORGE VANCOUVER (USA) *AidanO'Brien,Ireland* 2-8-10	RyanMoore (3)	93/10		1
	NOBLE TUNE (USA) *ChadCBrown,USA* 2-8-10	RamonADominguez (9)	39/10f	1¼	2
	BALANCE THE BOOKS (USA) *ChadCBrown,USA* 2-8-10	JulienRLeparoux (8)	98/10	nk	3
5894[2]	Dundonnell (USA) *RogerCharlton,GB* 2-8-10	JamesDoyle (6)	49/10	1¼	4
	Gervinho (USA) *CarlaGaines,USA* 2-8-10	RafaelBejarano (4)	98/10	hd	5
6303[2]	Artigiano (USA) *MahmoodAlZarooni,GB* 2-8-10	FrankieDettori (2)	61/10	3	6
6648*	Lines of Battle (USA) *AidanO'Brien,Ireland* 2-8-10 (b)	RichardHughes (14)	276/10	nk	7
6515*	Joha (USA) *MichaelJMaker,USA* 2-8-10	JavierCastellano (10)	92/10	¾	8
	Brown Almighty (USA) *TimAlce,USA* 2-8-10	KentJDesormeaux (7)	181/10	¾	9
6303[5]	Fantastic Moon *JeremyNoseda,GB* 2-8-10	KierenFallon (5)	124/10	1¼	10
6348	Dry Summer (USA) *JeffMullins,USA* 2-8-10	JosephTalamo (11)	236/10	1	11
	Summit County (USA) *DaleLRomans,USA* 2-8-10	CoreySNakatani (1)	558/10	1¼	12
6348[2]	Know More (USA) *DougFO'Neill,USA* 2-8-10	GarrettKGomez (13)	184/10	1¾	13
	I'm Boundtoscore (USA) *TroyRankin,USA* 2-8-10	SarahRook (12)	435/10	hd	14

6.50race Mrs John Magnier,Mr M.Tabor & Mr D.Smith 14ran 1m33.78

European runners have a strong record in this event and one of the raiding party landed the spoils once more, George Vancouver getting the better of a domestically-trained pair, with the third-placed Balance The Books shaping as well as anything in the race; the early pace was strong before steadying somewhat, but that didn't prevent those ridden with some restraint from getting into the race. **George Vancouver**, on firmer ground than he has previously encountered, built on his creditable third in the Dewhurst last time to emerge on top after enjoying a nice trip through the race; after travelling well in touch on the inner, he made good headway 2f out and quickened through a narrow gap to lead inside the final 1f, driven out from there; the 2000 Guineas is a likely early-season target next year, though connections state that fast ground is important, and he'll need to improve to reverse Dewhurst form with Dawn Approach there. **Noble Tune** lost his unbeaten record, but improved slightly on the form of his decisive win in the Grade 3 Pilgrim Stakes last time, not as well drawn/positioned as the winner here, but not appealing as unlucky either; held up early, he made headway under pressure 2f out and chased the winner in the final 1f, keeping on without making any real impression; he appeals as the type to go on progressing next year. **Balance The Books** progressed again and indeed looked unlucky not to finish closer or even win; in rear early, he travelled well and made headway over 2f out, but then had no room and was forced to switch 1f out, losing any chance of winning but finishing really well once in the clear; he remains open to improvement and is an exciting prospect for next year. **Dundonnell** failed to progress on his most recent efforts in bare form terms, but that doesn't tell the

whole story, little going right for him here and again leaving the impression that he may yet do better; after racing freely in mid-field and running wide on the first bend, he travelled strongly and made good headway 3f out, then having to be reined back before quickening up to challenge over 1f out, weakening in the closing stages as his earlier exertions told; there's every chance he'll line up in the 2000 Guineas next spring, though with his pedigree and style of racing it wouldn't be a surprise if he proved suited by 6f/7f; either way he remains an interesting prospect. **Artigiano** arrived on the back of a good effort when runner-up in the Royal Lodge, but wasn't in the same form here, he was a touch slowly away and, despite keeping on steadily, was never able to get into the race. **Lines of Battle**, in first-time blinkers (replacing cheekpieces) and tackling a 1f longer trip, shaped better than the bare result; he was rushed up early from his wide draw and raced freely on the outer, but stayed on terms with the principals until weakening in the final 1f as his earlier exertions told; he boasts a generally progressive profile and may do better still next year. **Fantastic Moon** is better judged on previous form, blowing his chance with a slow start here and never able to get into the race after; it would be no surprise to see him resume his progress next year, when he should prove suited by 1¼m.

SAINT-CLOUD Saturday, Nov 10
HEAVY

7261 Criterium de Saint-Cloud (Gr 1) (2yo c+f) £114,280 1¼m

6867*	MORANDI (FR) *Jean-ClaudeRouget,France* 2-9-0 MaximeGuyon	7/10f	1
6877*	WILLIE THE WHIPPER *AnnDuffield,GB* 2-9-0 JamieSpencer	35/10	7 2
6483²	MISS YOU TOO *DavidSimcock,GB* 2-8-11 (h) IanMongan	18/1	3 3
	Sempre Medici (FR) *MmeMBollack-Badel,France* 2-9-0 AlexBadel	14/1	1 4
3491*	Kapstadt (FR) *FrancoisDoumen,France* 2-9-0 UmbertoRispoli	11/1	nk 5
6928⁵	Cassiopee (FR) *YBarberot,France* 2-8-11 AntoineHamelin	31/1	4 6
	Princedargent (FR) *H-APantall,France* 2-9-0 OlivierPeslier	19/1	12 7
6904*	Wingate *H-APantall,France* 2-9-0 FabriceVeron	85/10	dist 8

Mr D-Y. Treves 8ran 2m25.30

Just a useful field on balance but it at least gave a bit more substance to Morandi's claims to being one of the season's leading two-year-olds as he strolled away with his second wide-margin win of the autumn; this was a real test of stamina for youngsters, particularly after Wingate, who paid the price later on, strung them out in the early stages before the pace steadied, the time still the quickest of the 4 races on the card at this trip. **Morandi**'s wide-margin win in the Prix de Conde lacked substance but he confirmed that form with another easy victory, this time over a field with more strength to it; he chased the leader, was travelling well when taking over soon after the home turn and once shaken up went clear from 2f out, running on strongly before coasting home; he'll stay 1½m next year, and clearly revels in the mud, though it remains to be seen whether he'll prove as effective on better ground. **Willie The Whipper**, supplemented for this and stepped up another 2f in trip, improved again; in touch in third, he tracked the leaders on the home turn and stayed on in the straight, pulling clear of the rest but no match for the winner; he'll stay 1½m, though even more so than the winner he's an unknown quantity away from heavy ground. **Miss You Too** ran creditably over this longer trip and saw it out surprisingly well despite another headstrong display; held up but refusing to settle, she plugged on in the straight; she's bred to stay 1½m, though her chances of doing so will be improved if she settles down a bit next year.

OPEN ACCESS FROM £2.50 A DAY

Race Passes are the ultimate form guide, featuring ratings, Horses In Focus, Warning Horses, In-Play Hints and symbols, live Betfair prices – plus unlimited use of a 12-year archive and Horse Searches.

Subscriptions give you open access to Timeform data for every meeting in Britain and Ireland plus big races abroad, starting from just £10 for 24 hours, to £70 per month by Direct Debit. That's less than £2.50 per day.

It's like a Form Book, Black Book & Race Card all in one!

Race Passes

Ratings. Form. In-Play. Betfair prices.
Search any horse, any race, any time.

ONLY AVAILABLE AT
timeform.com

TIMEFORM
THE HOME OF WINNERS SINCE 1948

TIMEFORM'S BEST OF 2012

Juveniles

The Irish-trained **Dawn Approach** (126p) was Timeform's highest-rated two-year-old in the world in 2012, following a campaign in which he was unbeaten in six races, the last two of them Group 1s at the Curragh (National Stakes) and Newmarket (Dewhurst Stakes). He accounted for stablemate **Leitir Mor** (117) readily by two and three quarter lengths in the latter, with **George Vancouver** (116) a further three quarters of a length back in third. The subsequent success of the latter in the Breeders' Cup Juvenile Turf at Santa Anita franked the Dewhurst form and saw Dawn Approach's rating rise further. Dawn Approach's rating is the joint-fourth-highest by a champion two-year-old this century, behind Frankel (133p in 2010), New Approach (127 in 2007 and, like his son Dawn Approach, trained by Jim Bolger) and Johannesburg (127 in 2001). The 'p' symbol on Dawn Approach's rating indicates the expectation of further improvement from him at three years.

Aidan O'Brien's **Kingsbarns** (120p) is clear favourite for the 2013 Derby at Epsom, following wins in a maiden at Navan and the Racing Post Trophy at Doncaster, the latter coming by one and three quarter lengths and a short head from **Van Der Neer** (115) and **Steeler** (115). Kingsbarn's rating is 3 lb higher than Camelot's was at the end of his juvenile campaign, with the pair having very similar profiles.

Remarkably, no British-trained juvenile made the top ten in our two-year-old Global Rankings, an indicator of another below-par year in the division domestically. The highest-rated British juvenile was the Prix Morny and Middle Park Stakes winner **Reckless Abandon**, whose 117 rating has been surpassed by the British juvenile champion in every intervening year since 1997. May Hill and Fillies' Mile winner **Certify** was the highest-rated British-trained two-year-old filly on 113.

Shanghai Bobby (123) led the way in the states, his unbeaten five-race campaign culminating with the Breeders' Cup Juvenile at Santa Anita. That race was run at an overly-strong gallop, in which he only just hung on from **He's Had Enough** (118).

Sprinters

There is no mistaking where the best sprinters in the world are currently to be found: five of the top six ratings in this category in 2012 were for horses trained in Australia or originating from there.

Leading the way was **Black Caviar** (136), who extended her unbeaten run to twenty-two in unforgettable fashion in the Diamond Jubilee Stakes at Royal Ascot. It was not her hard-fought victory over subsequent Prix Maurice de Gheest winner

Black Caviar (salmon with black dots) scraping home at Royal Ascot

Moonlight Cloud (126) and **Restiadargent** (120) that day that earned her a rating of 136, however: far from it, as Black Caviar ran to only 123. Better efforts had come on her home turf, and particularly in the Lightning Stakes at Flemington in February, when she accounted for **Hay List** (132) readily by one and three quarter lengths. Black Caviar is not only exceptional by sprinting standards, but also in historical terms; she is the joint-highest-rated filly or mare aged three or above in Timeform's sixty-five-year history, on a par with Allez France (the French-trained Arc winner in 1974) and Habibti (the outstanding British-trained sprinter of 1983).

Another Australian-trained mare that had notable success on these shores in 2012 was **Ortensia** (123), who landed the King George Stakes at Goodwood and the Nunthorpe Stakes at York. **Little Bridge** (126) was another winning raider of a major British prize, his King's Stand victory by three quarters of a length over **Bated Breath** (123) confirming the best rating he had registered back home in Hong Kong.

British-trained sprinters were plentiful in number but lacking in star quality, **Society Rock** (126) running to his best just once, when winning the Sprint Cup at Haydock, but nonetheless edging the title of best sprinter trained in Britain throughout 2012. The mud-loving **Mayson** (124) was the beneficiary of a wet summer as he landed the other big sprint prize in Britain, the July Cup at Newmarket, before finding only the French-trained filly **Wizz Kid** (122) a neck too good in the Prix de l'Abbaye at Longchamp.

Most of the top US-trained sprinters won in turn, an exception being **Groupie Doll** (128), who landed five in a row in blinkers between six and seven furlongs, culminating in a clear-cut success in the Breeders' Cup Filly & Mare Sprint. Her rating makes her joint-highest US-trained female with the middle-distance filly Royal Delta.

Milers

One man's blessing is all other milers' curse, and the phenomenal **Frankel** cast a giant shadow over the division. A rating of 147, achieved when he beat Excelebration by eleven lengths in the Queen Anne Stakes at Royal Ascot, is the highest mark awarded to any horse ever assessed by Timeform. Frankel was untouchable over a mile, and the three Group 1s he contested at that distance in 2012 he won by a combined total of twenty-two lengths.

Frankel moving up in trip at the end of his career gave centre stage to **Excelebration** (133) in Europe, and he didn't fluff his lines, underlining what a top miler he is in his own right with wins in the Prix Jacques Le Marois at Deauville (by one and three quarter lengths from **Cityscape** (126), with unlucky-in-running **Moonlight Cloud** close behind in fourth) and the QEII at Ascot, in which he beat Cityscape all the more convincingly by three lengths. Moonlight Cloud made amends in the Prix du Moulin at Longchamp where she narrowly got the better of Farhh (128), who had been through the Frankel mill when runner-up to that rival on his two preceding starts.

However, there was something of a miling sensation in America too, on turf surprisingly, and when Excelebration and Moonlight Cloud travelled over for the

Frankel slamming his rivals in the Queen Anne

Breeders' Cup Mile they were well and truly put in their place by **Wise Dan** (134). Admittedly, the European pair weren't near their best at Santa Anita, but Wise Dan had already produced marginally better performances than Excelebration through the year, notably when he ran away with a Grade 3 at Keeneland (by ten lengths, on polytrack) and when he made short work of a Grade 1 field that included Cityscape in the Woodbine Mile.

Middle Distances

Brilliance knows no boundaries, and the imperious **Frankel** straddles both the mile and middle-distance divisions. The highest-rated horse in Timeform's history, Frankel proved equally as outstanding over ten furlongs as shorter when given the opportunity on his final two appearances. Frankel's swansong came in the Champion Stakes at Ascot, where the testing ground prevented him from really turning it on in the way he almost always did, but he still readily defeated the second-best middle-distance horse in the world, **Cirrus des Aigles** (135), by one and three quarter lengths, with Eclipse winner **Nathaniel** (129) a further two and a half lengths away in third. On firmer going, on his first attempt beyond a mile, Frankel had produced an awesome performance to slam Farhh and **St Nicholas**

Abbey (127) by seven lengths, without looking extended, in the Juddmonte International at York.

In terms of the three-year-olds, the States had better middle-distance performers than the Europeans, and both **I'll Have Another** (130) and **Bodemeister** (129) might have achieved even higher ratings but for the injuries that prematurely ended their careers in May. I'll Have Another beat Bodemeister into second in both the Kentucky Derby and the Preakness Stakes, and the Triple Crown—not completed in America since 1978—looked at the mercy of I'll Have Another until a tendon problem just days before the Belmont.

Remarkably, bucking a long-standing trend, there was a Triple Crown attempt in Britain in 2012, for the first time in forty-two years. Having won the 2000 Guineas and the Derby (the best performance by a three-year-old over any distance in Europe in 2012), **Camelot** (128) could manage only second in the St Leger, then blotted his copybook further still when down the field in the Arc, a race memorable for Japanese raider Orfevre (130) snatching defeat from the jaws of victory. Orfevre went closer still in the Japan Cup, beaten a nose when conceding 9 lb to three-year-old filly **Gentildonna** (127), but that effort, coupled with a smooth success in the Group 1 Takarazuka Kinen earlier in the season, cemented his status as the top horse in Japan for the second year running.

Beaten favourite in the Dubai World Cup won by **Monterosso** (128), **So You Think** (132) bounced back and looked as good as ever with two wins, including the Prince of Wales's Stakes at Royal Ascot, before his retirement to stud. So You Think was a globetrotter but made his name in Australia, much like **Dunaden** (130) has, and the former Melbourne Cup winner achieved an even higher rating in 2012, again in Australia, where he defied top weight in the Caulfield Cup.

Last but not least, a word on the fillies. America's finest, **Royal Delta** (128), made it back-to-back wins in the Breeders' Cup Ladies Classic, while **Snow Fairy** (128) showed equivalent form landing the Irish Champion Stakes, and it would be remiss not to mention **Danedream** (126), the King George winner (in a tight finish with Nathaniel) who was prevented from defending her Arc de Triomphe title by a travel embargo after a case of swamp fever was found near her base in Germany.

Stayers

There has been a definite improvement in quality in recent years in the Melbourne Cup, and worldwide this seems to have now become the key race in the calendar for stayers. 2011 winner Americain might only have finished eleventh in 2012, but in a modestly-run contest he wasn't beaten far from a high mark, posting a

Timeform rating of 125, a match for third-placed **Jakkalberry** and, despite not winning, these were the joint-best performances of the year in a staying race on our figures. **Green Moon** (124) was the winner that day, in receipt of 10 lb and 4 lb respectively from the aforementioned pair, whilst **Fiorente** (123) finished second, beaten a length by Green Moon off the same mark. **Mount Athos** (124, caught the eye in fifth, finishing strongly having not had the run of the race) and **Dunaden** (fourteenth off top weight) are the others that ran in the Melbourne Cup and feature in the top stayers list.

Encke beating Camelot in the St Leger

Another race in which the gallop wasn't strong and they finished bunched up was the Ascot Gold Cup, Britain's top staying race, in prestige at least, though in this instance over two and a half miles on good to soft ground it's fair to say that there was still an emphasis on stamina. The race was won by **Colour Vision**, who ran to a Timeform rating of 121 in beating **Opinion Poll** (120) by half a length, though his best performance in ratings terms had come a bit earlier in the season, when landing the two-mile Sagaro Stakes on Kempton's polytrack surface. **Encke** (123) fared best of the three-year-olds courtesy of his win in the St Leger at Doncaster, when beating a below-par Camelot.

2012 STATISTICS

TRAINERS (1,2,3 earnings)	Horses	Indiv'l Wnrs	Races Won	Runs	Strike Rate	Stakes £
1 John Gosden	166	89	119	629	18.9	3,505,346
2 Aidan O'Brien, Ireland	37	12	13	73	17.8	3,455,710
3 Richard Hannon	283	142	218	1367	15.9	2,633,615
4 Sir Henry Cecil	85	38	56	289	19.3	2,514,709
5 Mark Johnston	211	111	215	1344	15.9	2,119,693
6 Richard Fahey	235	98	142	1294	10.9	1,774,187
7 Saeed bin Suroor	125	59	85	436	19.4	1,728,762
8 Andrew Balding	161	69	93	712	13.0	1,234,111
9 Kevin Ryan	154	63	95	789	12.0	1,120,444
10 William Haggas	107	58	83	448	18.5	1,112,131

JOCKEYS (by winners)	1st	2nd	3rd	Unpl	Total Rides	Strike Rate
1 Joe Fanning	188	150	118	683	1139	16.5
2 Richard Hughes	177	141	92	449	859	20.6
3 Luke Morris	159	188	175	811	1529	10.3
4 Jim Crowley	148	103	81	517	849	17.4
5 Silvestre de Sousa	145	118	125	593	981	14.8
6 William Buick	130	85	99	382	696	18.7
7 Paul Hanagan	122	92	101	486	801	15.2
8 Adam Kirby	119	112	91	426	748	15.9
9 Ryan Moore	116	87	81	319	603	19.2
10 Graham Lee	108	111	87	587	893	12.0

SIRES OF WINNERS (1,2,3 earnings)	Races Won	Runs	Strike Rate	£
1 Galileo (by Sadler's Wells)	85	448	18.9	4,017,720
2 Montjeu (by Sadler's Wells)	51	398	12.8	2,229,173
3 Exceed And Excel (by Danehill)	107	842	12.7	1,884,261
4 Invincible Spirit (by Green Desert)	95	772	12.3	1,627,382
5 Pivotal (by Polar Falcon)	103	780	13.2	1,465,505
6 Dansili (by Danehill)	75	527	14.2	1,378,189
7 Dubawi (by Dubai Millennium)	76	479	15.8	1,047,915
8 Oasis Dream (by Green Desert)	126	932	13.5	1,046,011
9 Selkirk (by Sharpen Up)	40	327	12.2	841,281
10 Cape Cross (by Green Desert)	108	821	13.1	825,232

LEADING HORSES (1,2,3 earnings)	Races Won	Runs	£
1 Frankel 4 b.c Galileo – Kind	5	5	1,625,593
2 Camelot 3 b.c Montjeu – Tarfah	2	3	1,083,171
3 Excelebration 4 b.c Exceed And Excel – Sun Shower	1	3	679,975
4 Nathaniel 4 b.c Galileo – Magnificient Style	1	3	596,465
5 Danedream 4 b.f Lomitas – Danedrop	1	1	567,100
6 Farhh 4 b.c Pivotal – Gonbarda	1	5	382,413
7 Main Sequence 3 ch.g Aldebaran – Iktat	2	5	362,595
8 St Nicholas Abbey 5 b.h Montjeu – Leaping Water	1	3	355,740
9 Encke 3 b.c Kingmambo – Shawanda	2	4	348,585
10 Mayson 4 b.c Invincible Spirit – Mayleaf	3	6	309,785

SECTION

THE TIMEFORM TOP 100

2 YEAR OLDS

126p	Dawn Approach
123	Shanghai Bobby
120p	Kingsbarns
117	Leitir Mor
117	Morandi
117	Reckless Abandon
116p	Battle of Marengo
116p	Moohaajim
116	George Vancouver
116	Olympic Glory
115	Flotilla
115	Gale Force Ten
115	Steeler
115	Van Der Neer
114p	Cristoforo Colombo
114	Parliament Square
113p	Loch Garman
113p	Tawhid
113p	Toronado
113	Certify
113	Sugar Boy
112p	Big Break
112	Anna's Pearl
112	Artigiano
112	Indian Jade
112	Newfangled
112	Purr Along
112	Sky Lantern
112	Viztoria
112	Watsdachances
111	Dundonnell
111	Penny's Picnic
111	Sir Prancealot
111	Trading Leather
110	Grafelli
109p	Ghurair
109p	Law Enforcement
109p	Montiridge

109p	Rosdhu Queen
109p	Taayel
109	Bungle Inthejungle
109	First Cornerstone
109	Havana Gold
109	My Special J's
109	Rising Legend
109	What A Name
108p	Silasol
108	Glass Office
108	Hajam
108	Harasiya
108	Heavy Metal
108	Ian's Dream
108	Morawij
108	Probably
107p	Lines of Battle
107p	Tasaday
107	Ashdan
107	Ceiling Kitty
107	Invincible Warrior
107	Maureen
107	Pedro The Great
107	The Gold Cheongsam
106	Afonso De Sousa
106	Body And Soul
106	Designs On Rome
106	Garswood
106	Hototo
106	Master of War
106	Pearl Flute
106	Sound of Guns
106	Victrix Ludorum
106	Willie The Whipper
105p	Cocktail Queen
105p	Just The Judge
105p	Tamarkuz
105	Alhebayeb
105	Blaine
105	Cay Verde

105	Emell
105	Flying The Flag
105	Move To Strike
105	Orgilgo Bay
105	Sendmylovetorose
105	Tha'ir
105	Waterway Run
104P	Mars
104	Birdman
104	Boomshackerlacker
104	Deauville Prince
104	Fantastic Moon
104	Pay Freeze
104	Professor
104	Scintillula
104	Three Sea Captains
103p	Al Waab
103p	So Beloved
103	Ahern
103	Baileys Jubilee
103	Hoyam
103	Lewisham
103	Light Up My Life
103	Maxentius
103	Nargys
103	Pure Excellence
103	Sorella Bella
103	The Taj
103	Winning Express

3 YEAR OLDS

130	I'll Have Another
129	Bodemeister
128	Camelot
127	Gentildonna
127	Gold Ship
124	Pastorius
124	Union Rags
123	Encke

123	Novellist
123	The Fugue
122	Caspar Netscher
122	French Fifteen
122	Imperial Monarch
122	Ridasiyna
122	Saonois
121	Fallen For You
121	Mince
121	Saint Baudolino
120	Aesop's Fables
120	Bayrir
120	Cogito
120	Elusive Kate
120	Girolamo
120	Grandeur
120	Great Heavens
120	Homecoming Queen
120	Restiadargent
120	Valyra
119	Astrology
119	Feuerblitz
119	Fulbright
119	Hartani
119	Main Sequence
119	Masterstroke
119	Most Improved
119	Princess Highway
119	Thought Worthy
118	Beauty Parlour
118	Bonfire
118	Deep Brillante
118	Last Train
118	Lethal Force
118	Noble Mission
118	Offer
118	Speaking of Which
118	Ursa Major
117	Akeed Mofeed
117	Aljamaaheer

117	All Shamar	114	Brendan Brackan	125	Capponi	120	Fame And Glory
117	Archbishop	114	Caponata	125	Jakkalberry	120	Galikova
117	Bannock	114	Dabirsim	125	Rocket Man	120	Harris Tweed
117	Born To Sea	114	Dragon Pulse	124	Famous Name	120	Hitchens
117	Duntle	114	Energizer	124	Green Moon	120	Maarek
117	Ektihaam	114	Foxtrot Romeo	124	Mayson	120	Mikhail Glinka
117	Gregorian	114	Guarantee	124	Mount Athos	120	Mull of Killough
117	Hermival	114	Gusto	124	Reliable Man	120	Opinion Poll
117	Massiyn	114	Les Beaufs	124	Solemia	120	Penitent
117	Michelangelo	114	Lucayan	123	Bated Breath	120	Saamidd
117	Power	114	Shantaram	123	Carlton House	120	Saddler's Rock
117	Thomas Chippendale	114	Van Ellis	123	Chinchon	120	Sapphire
117	Trumpet Major			123	Colour Vision	120	Temida
117	Voleuse De Coeurs	**OLDER HORSES**		123	Fiorente	120	The Reaper
117	Was			123	Gordon Lord Byron	120	Tiddliwinks
117	Yellow And Green	147	Frankel	123	Musir	120	Tin Horse
117	Yellow Rosebud	136	Black Caviar	123	Ortensia	120	Worthadd
116p	Declaration of War	135	Cirrus Des Aigles	123	Spirit Quartz	120	Zinabaa
116	Chamonix	134	Wise Dan	122	Fox Hunt	119	Afsare
116	Daddy Long Legs	133	Excelebration	122	Golden Lilac	119	Captain Ramius
116	Gamilati	132	Hay List	122	Hamish Mcgonagall	119	Dandino
116	Pearl Mix	132	So You Think	122	Joy And Fun	119	Dandy Boy
116	Repeater	130	Dunaden	122	No Risk At All	119	Delegator
116	Rougemont	130	Orfevre	122	Ovambo Queen	119	Do It All
116	Sagawara	129	Ambitious Dragon	122	Planteur	119	Giofra
116	Samitar	129	Nathaniel	122	Prince Bishop	119	Highland Knight
116	Shirocco Star	129	Sepoy	122	Shareta	119	I'm A Dreamer
116	Sovereign Debt	128	Farhh	122	Sole Power	119	Joshua Tree
116	Swiss Spirit	128	Monterosso	122	Soul	119	Krypton Factor
116	Up	128	Royal Delta	122	Twice Over	119	Libranno
115	Cameron Highland	128	Snow Fairy	122	Wizz Kid	119	Mendip
115	Fire Lily	127	Americain	121	Albaasil	119	Mutahadee
115	I Have A Dream	127	Sea Moon	121	Crackerjack King	119	Nahrain
115	Lady Wingshot	127	St Nicholas Abbey	121	Ivory Land	119	Premio Loco
115	Laugh Out Loud	126	California Memory	121	Izzi Top	119	Side Glance
115	Light Heavy	126	Cityscape	121	Master of Hounds	119	Siyouma
115	Lockwood	126	Danedream	121	Red Cadeaux	119	Time Prisoner
115	Mashoora	126	Krypton Factor	121	Sharestan	119	Tullius
115	Producer	126	Little Bridge	121	Shimraan		
115	Requisition	126	Meandre	121	Skilful		
115	Starboard	126	Moonlight Cloud	121	Viscount Nelson		
115	Stipulate	126	Society Rock	120§	Sri Putra		
114p	Biographer	125	African Story	120	Aaim To Prosper		
114	Aklan	125	Al Kazeem	120	Brown Panther		

PROMISING HORSES

A p symbol is used by Timeform to denote horses we believe are capable of improvement, with a P symbol suggesting a horse is capable of much better form. Below is a list of selected British- and Irish-trained horses with a p or P, listed under their current trainers.

GEORGE BAKER

Aussie Lyrics (FR)	3 gr.c	81p

ANDREW BALDING

Absolutely So (IRE)	3 b.c	87p
Butterfly McQueen (USA)	3 b.f	80p
Daylight	3 ch.g	89p
Desert Command	3 b.g	76p
El Buen Turista	3 b.c	100p
Havana Beat (IRE)	3 b.c	91p
Here Comes When (IRE)	3 b.c	89p
Melvin The Grate (IRE)	3 b.c	82p
Mr Fitzroy (IRE)	3 ch.g	83p
Ningara	3 b.g	82p
Pearl Castle (IRE)	3 b.c	87p
Race And Status (IRE)	3 b.c	96p
Soviet Rock (IRE)	3 b.c	84p
Van Percy	3 b.g	86p

DAVID BARRON

Robot Boy (IRE)	3 ch.g	73p
Pearl Secret	4 ch.c	119p

RALPH BECKETT

Inka Surprise (IRE)	3 b.g	87p
Lemon Pearl	3 ch.f	80p
Pearl Bridge	3 b.g	80p
Secret Gesture	3 b.f	93p
Talent	3 ch.f	83p

MICHAEL BELL

Azrur (IRE)	3 b.c	86p
Fils Anges (IRE)	3 gr.c	89p
Huntsmans Close	3 b.g	92p
Madame Defarge (IRE)	3 b.f	84p
The Lark	3 ch.f	91p

JAMES BETHELL

Steelriver (IRE)	3 b.g	92p

J. S. BOLGER, IRELAND

Dawn Approach (IRE)	3 ch.c	126p
Loch Garman (IRE)	3 b.c	113p

MARCO BOTTI

Moohaajim (IRE)	3 b.c	116p
Guest of Honour (IRE)	4 b.c	95p

DAVID BROWN

Hollowina	3 ch.f	83p

HENRY CANDY

Code of Honor	3 b.c	98p
Pedro Serrano (IRE)	3 b.c	80p

SIR HENRY CECIL

Al Waab (IRE)	3 ch.c	103p
Autun (USA)	3 b.c	83p
Flow (USA)	3 b.c	88p
Hot Snap	3 ch.f	84p
Kyllachy Rise	3 b.c	82p
Mighty Yar (IRE)	3 gr.c	83p
Rome	3 b.c	83p
Squire Osbaldeston (IRE)	3 b.c	80p
Chigun	4 b.f	107p
Tiger Cliff (IRE)	4 b.g	96p

MICK CHANNON

Amralah (IRE)	3 b.c	86p
Enaitch (IRE)	3 gr.f	80p

PETER CHAPPLE-HYAM

Arbeel	3 b.f	83p

ROGER CHARLTON

Don Marco	3 b.g	90p
Greenery (IRE)	3 b.f	81p
Magog	3 br.g	84P
So Beloved	3 b.c	103p
Tartary (IRE)	3 b.c	81p
Bishop Roko	4 b.g	109p
Border Legend	4 ch.g	94p
Captain Cat (IRE)	4 b.g	100p
Clowance Estate (IRE)	4 b.g	86p
Valiant Girl	4 b.f	93p
Waterclock (IRE)	4 ch.g	88p

DENIS COAKLEY

Royal Dutch	4 ch.g	83p

PAUL COLE

Kuantan One (IRE)	3 b.c	83p
St Paul de Vence (IRE)	3 b.c	80p

CLIVE COX

Haafaguinea	3 ch.c	94p
Roanne (USA)	3 b.f	69p
Dance Express (IRE)	4 b.f	80p

LUCA CUMANI

Ajman Bridge	3 ch.c	90p

Elhaame (IRE)	3 b.g	85p
Greatwood	3 b.c	93p
Havana Cooler (IRE)	3 ch.c	85p
Hippy Hippy Shake	4 b.f	100p
Mallory Heights	3 b.c	75p
Rockalong (IRE)	4 b.c	90p

KEITH DALGLEISH

Hanalei Bay (IRE)	3 b.c	82p

TOM DASCOMBE

Ice Pie	3 b.f	85p
Saga Lout	3 b.g	81p

MICHAEL DODS

Dos Amigos (IRE)	4 b.g	91p

ED DUNLOP

Auction (IRE)	3 b.f	88p
Bowland Princess	3 b.f	63p
Contributer (IRE)	3 b.c	86p
Gworn	3 b.c	87p
Red Avenger (USA)	3 b.c	99p
Singersongwriter	3 ch.f	81p
Homeric (IRE)	4 b.g	87p

DAVID ELSWORTH

Cocktail Queen (IRE)	3 b.f	105p
Dashing Star	3 b.c	92p

RICHARD FAHEY

Asgardella	3 b.f	83p
Gabrial's Kaka (IRE)	3 b.g	94p
Heaven's Guest (IRE)	3 b.g	84p
Majestic Moon	3 b.g	86p
Mystery Bet (IRE)	3 b.f	88p
Romantic Settings	3 ch.f	80p
Unsinkable (IRE)	3 gr.c	92p

JAMES FANSHAWE

Ribbons	3 ch.f	84p
Eagle Power (IRE)	4 b.g	80p
Miss Dashwood	4 b.f	85p
Seal of Approval	4 b.f	95p
Villoresi (IRE)	4 b.g	82p

ED DE GILES

Twenty One Choice (IRE)	4 ch.g	81p

JOHN GOSDEN

Blessington (IRE)	3 b.c	93p
Bright Strike (USA)	3 b.c	88p
Chat (USA)	3 b.f	89p
Ghurair (USA)	3 b.c	109p
Khobaraa	3 b.f	82p
Khudoua	3 b.g	80p
Nichols Canyon	3 b.c	90p
Nickels And Dimes (IRE)	3 b.f	83p
Rottingdean	3 gr.c	81p
Seek Again (USA)	3 ch.c	96p
Sillabub (USA)	3 b.f	87p
Snow King (USA)	3 ch.c	96p
Space Ship	3 ch.c	82p
Taayel (IRE)	3 b.c	109p
Vanity Rules	3 b.f	85p
Winsili	3 b.f	101p
Hanseatic	4 b.c	95p
Nabucco	4 b.c	100p
Rippled	4 gr.f	82p
Tempest Fugit (IRE)	4 b.f	103p
Utterance	4 b.g	86p
Willow Beck	4 b.f	82p
Eshtibaak (IRE)	5 b.c	95p

RAE GUEST

Million Faces	4 ch.f	81p

WILLIAM HAGGAS

Crop Report (USA)	3 b.c	88p
I Say (IRE)	3 b.f	86p
Lady Nouf	3 b.f	89p
Leitrim Pass (USA)	3 ch.c	80p
Mundahesh (IRE)	3 ch.g	91p
Our Obsession (IRE)	3 ch.f	87p
Rosdhu Queen (IRE)	3 b.f	109p
Veeraya	3 b.g	87p
Danchai	4 gr.g	95p
Fast Or Free	4 ch.g	105p
Mukhadram	4 b.c	109p
Nine Realms	4 b.g	102p
Stencive	4 b.c	109p

RICHARD HANNON

Absolutely Right (IRE)	3 b.f	82p
Amberley Heights (IRE)	3 b.f	84p
Beautiful View	3 ch.f	93p
Law Enforcement (IRE)	3 b.c	109p

Montiridge (IRE)	3 b.c	109p
Mutazamen	3 ch.c	93p
Pivotal Movement	3 ch.c	82p
Rundell	3 b.c	82p
The Gatling Boy (IRE)	3 ch.c	84p
Toronado (IRE)	3 b.c	113p
Wentworth (IRE)	3 b.c	102p
Zurigha (IRE)	3 b.f	90p
Belle de Crecy (IRE)	4 b.f	86p

CHARLES HILLS

Barbs Princess	3 ch.f	81p
Englishman	3 b.c	89p
Just The Judge (IRE)	3 b.f	105p
Kerbaaj (USA)	3 b.c	89p
Mojo Miss (IRE)	3 b.f	80p
Unmoothaj	3 b.c	84p
Margate	4 b.f	80p

JO HUGHES

Smart Spender (IRE)	3 b.g	80p

DEAN IVORY

Tropics (USA)	5 ch.g	93p

ALAN JARVIS

Sword In Hand	4 b.c	83p

MARK JOHNSTON

Mister Impatience	3 b.c	87p
Windhoek	3 b.c	97p
Star Lahib (IRE)	4 b.f	82p

WILLIAM KNIGHT

Keep The Secret	3 ch.f	84p

DAVID LANIGAN

Plutocracy (IRE)	3 b.c	65p
Portmonarch (IRE)	3 b.c	83p
Tinghir (IRE)	3 b.c	80p
Biographer	4 b.c	114p

NICK LITTMODEN

Living Leader	4 b.g	87p

ED MCMAHON

Secretinthepark	3 ch.c	91p

BRIAN MEEHAN

Chief Inspector (IRE)	3 b.g	84p
Correspondent	3 ch.c	97p
Granell (IRE)	3 ch.c	89p
Legal Waves (IRE)	3 b.c	90p
Lord of The Garter (IRE)	3 b.c	89p
Mujazif (IRE)	3 br.c	93p
Supernova Heights (IRE)	3 b.f	95p

J. S. MOORE

Bertie Royale	3 b.g	80p

HUGHIE MORRISON

Countryman	3 b.c	82p
Town Mouse	3 ch.g	60p

JEREMY NOSEDA

Consign	3 b.g	82p
Excuse To Linger	3 ch.c	86p
Homage (IRE)	3 b.c	88p
Prophets Pride	3 b.c	81p
Regal Silk	3 b.f	84p
Silver Dixie (USA)	3 br.c	81P
Sweet Deal (IRE)	3 gr.g	84p
Zamoyski	3 ch.g	88p
Livery (IRE)	4 gr.c	98p
Net Whizz (USA)	4 b.c	89p

AIDAN O'BRIEN, IRELAND

Battle of Marengo (IRE)	3 b.c	116p
Cristoforo Colombo (USA)	3 b.c	114p
Eye of The Storm (IRE)	3 ch.c	100p
Festive Cheer (FR)	3 b.c	97P
Forester	3 gr.c	93p
Foundry (IRE)	3 b.c	96p
Francis of Assisi (IRE)	3 b.c	97p
Hanky Panky (IRE)	3 ch.f	93p
Indian Chief (IRE)	3 b.c	87p
Kingsbarns (IRE)	3 b.c	120p
Leading Light (IRE)	3 b.c	88p
Lines of Battle (USA)	3 b.c	107p
Mars (IRE)	3 ch.c	104P
Sir Walter Scott (IRE)	3 b.c	92P
Theatre (IRE)	3 b.c	100P
The Ferryman (IRE)	3 b.c	91p
The United States (IRE)	3 ch.c	102P
The Vatican (IRE)	3 b.c	83p
Vinson Massif (USA)	3 ch.c	94p
Declaration of War (USA)	4 b.c	116p
Marchese Marconi (IRE)	4 b.c	92P
Sidereus Nuncius (IRE)	4 ch.c	84p

DAVID O'MEARA

Dick Bos	4 ch.g	96p
War Lord (IRE)	3 b.g	60p

P. J. PRENDERGAST, IRELAND

Seolan (IRE)	3 b.f	102p

SIR MARK PRESCOTT BT

Alcaeus	3 b.c	–p
Mutual Regard (IRE)	4 b.g	99p
Pallasator	4 b.g	108p

KEVIN RYAN

Burning Blaze	3 b.c	95p
Equity Risk (USA)	3 b.f	84p
George Rooke (IRE)	3 b.c	86p
Greeleys Love (USA)	3 ch.c	87p
Plunder	3 ch.c	85p

DAVID SIMCOCK

Breton Rock (IRE)	3 b.c	90p
Line of Reason (IRE)	3 br.c	83p
Stasio (USA)	3 b.c	92p
Castilo Del Diablo (IRE)	4 br.c	95p

Mean It	4 b.g	91p
White Nile (IRE)	4 b.c	89p

SIR MICHAEL STOUTE

Altharoos (IRE)	3 br.g	88p
Enobled	3 b.c	85p
Hillstar	3 b.c	97p
Liber Nauticus (IRE)	3 b.f	92P
Love Magic	3 b.f	85p
Mango Diva	3 b.f	83p
Persepolis (IRE)	3 b.c	83p
Russian Realm	3 b.c	86p
Telescope (IRE)	3 b.c	96p
Theodore Gericault (IRE)	3 b.g	82p
Caskelena (IRE)	4 b.f	84p
Dank	4 b.f	105p
Enrol	4 b.f	92p
Fleur de Cactus (IRE)	4 b.f	92p
Gospel Choir	4 ch.c	109p
Minoan Dancer (IRE)	4 b.f	85p
Modern Tutor	4 b.c	88p
Rye House (IRE)	4 b.c	104p
Eagles Peak	5 b.c	107p

SAEED BIN SUROOR

Al Jamal	3 b.f	82p
Arabian Skies (IRE)	3 b.c	82p
Excellent Result (IRE)	3 b.c	89p
Muhtaris (IRE)	3 b.c	80p
Ostaad (IRE)	3 b.c	91p
Secret Number	3 b.c	95P
Tamarkuz (USA)	3 ch.c	105p
Tarikhi (USA)	3 b.c	90p
Tawhid	3 gr.c	113p
Thouwra (IRE)	3 b.c	80p
Wadi Al Hattawi (IRE)	3 b.c	86p
Albasharah (USA)	4 b.f	93p
Ehtedaam (USA)	4 b.c	86p
Layali Dubai (USA)	4 b.f	94p
Tadmir (USA)	4 b.c	87p
Ustura (USA)	4 b.g	96p

JAMES TATE

Bin Singspiel	3 br.c	80p
El Manati (IRE)	3 b.f	101p

MARCUS TREGONING

Muharrer	4 b.g	91p
On My Own (TUR)	4 b.c	81p

ROGER VARIAN

Agerzam	3 br.c	93p
Bit of A Gift (FR)	3 b.c	89p
Chelwood Gate (IRE)	3 h.c	82p
Elkaayed (USA)	3 ch.c	90p
Qawaafy (USA)	3 b.f	82p
Ribaat (IRE)	3 b.c	92p
Soaring Spirits (IRE)	3 ch.g	82p
Rose Season	4 b.f	86p
Kota Sas (IRE)	5 b.g	87p

ED VAUGHAN

Solemn Oath (USA)	4 b.c	82p

DAVID WACHMAN, IRELAND

Galileo Rock (IRE)	3 ch.c	100p

ED WALKER

Glorious Protector (IRE)	3 b.c	78P
Surge Ahead (IRE)	3 b.c	84p

CHRIS WALL

Blessing Box	3 b.f	66p
Bassara (IRE)	4 b.f	88p

D. K. WELD, IRELAND

Big Break	3 b.f	112p

MICHAEL WIGHAM

Fairway To Heaven (IRE)	4 b.c	90p

MAHMOOD AL ZAROONI

Altruism (IRE)	3 b.c	92p
Cat O'Mountain (USA)	3 b.c	93p
Chesterfield (IRE)	3 ch.c	89p
Desert Blossom (IRE)	3 ch.f	101p
Great Timing (USA)	3 ch.f	86p
Improvisation (IRE)	3 b.c	96p
Kalispell (IRE)	3 b.f	90p
Layl (USA)	3 b.c	82p
Lord Provost (IRE)	3 b.c	80p
Newsreader (USA)	3 b.c	80p
Now Spun (USA)	3 b.c	87p
Personable	3 b.c	82p
Stamford	3 b.g	84p
Sugar House (USA)	3 ch.f	80p
Top Joker	3 b.c	84p
Valley of Queens (IRE)	3 ch.f	83p
Zurbriggen	3 ch.c	88p
Circus Mondao (USA)	4 b.g	91p
Mighty Ambition (USA)	4 b.c	83p
Prince of Orange (IRE)	4 b.c	85p
Punita (USA)	4 ch.f	91p

TRAINERS FOR COURSES

The following statistics show the most successful trainers over the past five seasons at each of the courses that stage Flat racing in England, Scotland and Wales.

ASCOT

Trainer	Wins	Runs	%	Trainer	Wins	Runs	%
Richard Hannon	27	341	8	William Haggas	18	129	14
Mark Johnston	26	299	9	Sir Henry Cecil	14	75	19
Aidan O'Brien, Ire	22	127	17	Saeed bin Suroor	13	134	10
John Gosden	22	158	14	Clive Cox	12	100	12
Sir Michael Stoute	21	145	14	Michael Bell	12	106	11

AYR

Trainer	Wins	Runs	%	Trainer	Wins	Runs	%
Richard Fahey	58	348	17	Kevin Ryan	19	181	10
Jim Goldie	47	534	9	Keith Dalgleish	17	92	18
Michael Dods	24	211	11	Alan Swinbank	15	86	17
Tim Easterby	22	128	17	David Nicholls	15	166	9
Linda Perratt	20	296	7	Alistair Whillans	14	77	18

BATH

Trainer	Wins	Runs	%	Trainer	Wins	Runs	%
Mick Channon	35	259	14	Brian Meehan	17	78	22
Richard Hannon	34	177	19	Malcolm Saunders	16	153	10
Andrew Balding	20	107	19	David Evans	16	165	10
Ron Hodges	19	178	11	Clive Cox	13	87	15
Ronald Harris	18	273	7	Milton Bradley	12	207	6

BEVERLEY

Trainer	Wins	Runs	%	Trainer	Wins	Runs	%
Mark Johnston	60	216	28	Mel Brittain	18	106	17
Richard Fahey	41	321	13	David Nicholls	17	126	13
Kevin Ryan	25	176	14	Bryan Smart	16	126	13
Tim Easterby	22	353	6	John Quinn	16	172	9
Paul Midgley	20	235	9	Ann Duffield	14	122	11

BRIGHTON

Trainer	Wins	Runs	%	Trainer	Wins	Runs	%
David Evans	22	153	14	Mark Johnston	13	55	24
Richard Hannon	21	105	20	Jim Best	12	43	28
David Simcock	18	57	32	Stuart Williams	12	54	22
Mick Channon	18	160	11	John Bridger	12	122	10
Gary Moore	18	178	10	Jeremy Noseda	11	29	38

CARLISLE

Trainer	Wins	Runs	%	Trainer	Wins	Runs	%
Richard Fahey	24	160	15	Alan Swinbank	9	106	8
Tim Easterby	23	154	15	Mark Johnston	8	61	13
Brian Ellison	13	65	20	David Nicholls	8	61	13
Kevin Ryan	13	67	19	Michael Easterby	8	70	11
Bryan Smart	9	61	15	Michael Dods	8	97	8

CATTERICK BRIDGE

Trainer	Wins	Runs	%	Trainer	Wins	Runs	%
David Nicholls	31	196	16	Geoffrey Harker	18	94	19
Tim Easterby	30	238	13	David O'Meara	17	100	17
Mark Johnston	27	144	19	Paul Midgley	16	169	9
Kevin Ryan	23	140	16	Ruth Carr	15	106	14
Richard Fahey	21	147	14	Brian Ellison	14	85	16

CHEPSTOW

Trainer	Wins	Runs	%	Trainer	Wins	Runs	%
Richard Hannon	19	117	16	Malcolm Saunders	13	61	21
Andrew Balding	16	66	24	Bernard Llewellyn	12	75	16
Ralph Beckett	14	59	24	Tony Carroll	11	120	9
Ronald Harris	14	184	8	David Evans	11	175	6
John Spearing	13	43	30	Bryn Palling	10	144	7

CHESTER

Trainer	Wins	Runs	%	Trainer	Wins	Runs	%
Mark Johnston	30	196	15	David Evans	14	185	8
Richard Fahey	29	236	12	Sir Michael Stoute	12	53	23
Andrew Balding	15	66	23	Mark Brisbourne	12	150	8
Kevin Ryan	15	113	13	Aidan O'Brien, Ire	11	26	42
Mick Channon	14	97	14	William Haggas	10	32	31

TRAINERS FOR COURSES

DONCASTER

Trainer	Wins	Runs	%	Trainer	Wins	Runs	%
Richard Fahey	38	374	10	Jeremy Noseda	17	87	20
Richard Hannon	33	192	17	Michael Bell	17	106	16
John Gosden	31	151	21	Saeed bin Suroor	17	112	15
Mark Johnston	22	250	9	Tim Easterby	17	275	6
Luca Cumani	18	88	20	Brian Meehan	14	79	18

EPSOM DOWNS

Trainer	Wins	Runs	%	Trainer	Wins	Runs	%
Richard Hannon	19	136	14	Mick Channon	11	116	9
Andrew Balding	18	85	21	Ralph Beckett	10	41	24
Mark Johnston	15	149	10	Simon Dow	8	65	12
Saeed bin Suroor	13	47	28	Pat Phelan	8	91	9
Sir Mark Prescott Bt	11	29	38	Sir Henry Cecil	7	36	19

FFOS LAS

Trainer	Wins	Runs	%	Trainer	Wins	Runs	%
David Evans	11	83	13	Rod Millman	6	48	13
David Simcock	10	36	28	Mick Channon	6	51	12
Mark Johnston	9	43	21	Ronald Harris	6	56	11
Brian Meehan	7	23	30	William Haggas	5	12	42
Richard Hannon	6	27	22	Ralph Beckett	5	17	29

GOODWOOD

Trainer	Wins	Runs	%	Trainer	Wins	Runs	%
Richard Hannon	85	525	16	Jeremy Noseda	19	82	23
Mark Johnston	32	220	15	Luca Cumani	19	89	21
Sir Michael Stoute	25	118	21	Sir Henry Cecil	17	81	21
John Gosden	20	135	15	Brian Meehan	17	108	16
Amanda Perrett	20	178	11	Mick Channon	17	287	6

HAMILTON PARK

Trainer	Wins	Runs	%	Trainer	Wins	Runs	%
Richard Fahey	51	230	22	Linda Perratt	22	322	7
Mark Johnston	50	235	21	David Nicholls	20	88	23
Kevin Ryan	35	160	22	Alan Swinbank	19	117	16
Jim Goldie	25	241	10	Tim Easterby	15	89	17
Bryan Smart	23	111	21	Eric Alston	13	72	18

HAYDOCK PARK

Trainer	Wins	Runs	%	Trainer	Wins	Runs	%
Richard Fahey	30	282	11	Richard Hannon	17	123	14
Tom Dascombe	27	117	23	William Haggas	16	55	29
Mark Johnston	22	244	9	John Gosden	16	76	21
Kevin Ryan	21	196	11	Ian Williams	16	103	16
David Nicholls	19	159	12	Alan Swinbank	15	93	16

KEMPTON PARK AW

Trainer	Wins	Runs	%	Trainer	Wins	Runs	%
Richard Hannon	126	878	14	Mark Johnston	58	420	14
Saeed bin Suroor	66	211	31	Tony Carroll	54	523	10
Andrew Balding	62	385	16	Ralph Beckett	53	257	21
Gary Moore	62	451	14	Jim Boyle	45	406	11
John Gosden	58	291	20	Marco Botti	42	292	14

LEICESTER

Trainer	Wins	Runs	%	Trainer	Wins	Runs	%
Richard Hannon	31	174	18	Ralph Beckett	13	61	21
Mark Johnston	28	138	20	Sir Michael Stoute	13	62	21
Saeed bin Suroor	15	41	37	Brian Meehan	13	67	19
Mick Channon	15	117	13	Kevin Ryan	12	80	15
Luca Cumani	13	53	25	David Evans	12	145	8

LINGFIELD PARK Turf

Trainer	Wins	Runs	%	Trainer	Wins	Runs	%
Richard Hannon	15	94	16	Sir Michael Stoute	9	37	24
Mick Channon	14	74	19	Roger Charlton	7	17	41
Sir Henry Cecil	11	36	31	Mahmood Al Zarooni	7	17	41
Gary Moore	11	72	15	Alan Jarvis	7	25	28
Rod Millman	10	48	21	Tony Carroll	7	41	17

LINGFIELD PARK AW

Trainer	Wins	Runs	%	Trainer	Wins	Runs	%
Mark Johnston	80	412	19	Jim Boyle	46	423	11
Richard Hannon	73	482	15	Jeremy Noseda	45	170	26
Gary Moore	72	545	13	Saeed bin Suroor	42	87	48
J. S. Moore	49	354	14	Ronald Harris	37	342	11
David Evans	49	476	10	Tom Dascombe	36	141	26

SANDOWN PARK

Trainer	Wins	Runs	%	Trainer	Wins	Runs	%
Richard Hannon	49	358	14	Jeremy Noseda	15	50	30
Sir Michael Stoute	38	181	21	William Haggas	15	67	22
John Gosden	29	173	17	Luca Cumani	11	73	15
Andrew Balding	22	150	15	Saeed bin Suroor	11	77	14
Mark Johnston	17	175	10	Sir Henry Cecil	10	61	16

SOUTHWELL AW

Trainer	Wins	Runs	%	Trainer	Wins	Runs	%
Mark Johnston	80	319	25	David Barron	53	220	24
Kevin Ryan	68	347	20	Richard Fahey	45	298	15
Brian Ellison	64	290	22	Bryan Smart	44	296	15
David Nicholls	60	301	20	Hughie Morrison	41	167	25
Alan McCabe	57	547	10	Paul Midgley	33	336	10

THIRSK

Trainer	Wins	Runs	%	Trainer	Wins	Runs	%
Richard Fahey	25	175	14	Mark Johnston	16	127	13
Tim Easterby	25	311	8	Ruth Carr	12	94	13
Kevin Ryan	24	191	13	Alan Swinbank	12	102	12
David Nicholls	24	224	11	David O'Meara	11	81	14
Michael Dods	17	165	10	David Barron	11	113	10

WARWICK

Trainer	Wins	Runs	%	Trainer	Wins	Runs	%
Mark Johnston	13	66	20	Andrew Balding	9	51	18
Sir Henry Cecil	11	25	44	David Evans	9	79	11
Richard Hannon	11	87	13	Mick Channon	8	81	10
Ed McMahon	9	28	32	Tom Dascombe	7	37	19
William Haggas	9	39	23	Ralph Beckett	7	46	15

WINDSOR

Trainer	Wins	Runs	%	Trainer	Wins	Runs	%
Richard Hannon	96	562	17	Andrew Balding	18	110	16
David Evans	29	248	12	Roger Charlton	13	81	16
Sir Michael Stoute	26	113	23	Saeed bin Suroor	12	51	24
Jeremy Noseda	21	76	28	John Gosden	12	72	17
Ralph Beckett	20	123	16	Hughie Morrison	12	115	10

WOLVERHAMPTON AW

Trainer	Wins	Runs	%	Trainer	Wins	Runs	%
Mark Johnston	102	477	21	Richard Fahey	63	517	12
David Evans	93	885	11	Tom Dascombe	61	330	18
Reg Hollinshead	70	638	11	Mark Brisbourne	55	661	8
Kevin Ryan	65	442	15	Derek Shaw	52	546	10
Marco Botti	64	313	20	Michael Easterby	49	391	13

YARMOUTH

Trainer	Wins	Runs	%	Trainer	Wins	Runs	%
Mark H. Tompkins	32	269	12	Peter Chapple-Hyam	18	88	20
Chris Wall	30	155	19	Sir Michael Stoute	18	91	20
Michael Bell	27	140	19	Mick Channon	18	163	11
John Gosden	26	114	23	Sir Mark Prescott Bt	16	66	24
William Haggas	20	116	17	Clive Brittain	16	128	13

YORK

Trainer	Wins	Runs	%	Trainer	Wins	Runs	%
Richard Fahey	54	552	10	Kevin Ryan	15	204	7
Tim Easterby	26	314	8	Mark Johnston	14	231	6
William Haggas	17	71	24	David Nicholls	13	177	7
Saeed bin Suroor	16	116	14	Mick Channon	12	107	11
Sir Michael Stoute	15	95	16	Sir Henry Cecil	11	59	19

INDEX TO PHOTOGRAGHS

INDEX

INDEX